DEAL WITH IT!

How to Stop Running from People, Problems, and Pressure

BRIAN LAHOUE

2019. Boston. The new authoritative guide to confrontation.
Copyright © 2018, by Brian Lahoue

ISBN: 978-1-7336274-1-2 Paperback
ISBN: 978-1-7336274-0-5 eBook

CONTENTS

CHAPTER 3: ROLES, REACTIONS, AND RESPONSES TO CONFLICT 48

CHAPTER 4: CONVERSION: DEVELOPING A BETTER LIFE 83

CHAPTER 5: ABOUT THAT CONVERSATION: HOW SHOULD WE CONFRONT 123

CHAPTER 6: SIMPLE STRATEGIES FOR EFFECTIVE CONFRONTATION 142

CHAPTER 7: CONTINUAL SELF-TRANSFORMATION 163

DEDICATION

For those of you who want so much to change, for you who
have been labeled, for you who are afraid to confront others -
this book is for you.

EPIGRAPH

We cannot change or determine what circumstance we may face; we can only decide how we will respond.

PREFACE

It was an early morning at the office when, while reading some article I can no longer recall, I felt the urgency to make a note of the simplistic improvement and advice I would give on the matter of having to confront someone. What followed was a mentioning of my points that evening to friends and family at dinner, whereby I was challenged to write this book. It seemed humorous to some that I would endeavor to author on such a topic, and yet quite evident to others. In the end, I saw a primary goal to be reached - to help those who so feared confrontation to see that it is essential and can become more natural. A secondary goal also emerged - one which is very near to my heart. This goal is to champion the idea that everyone and anyone can change, and because of this, we should not be too quick to disparage and label others with terms that will only make change more doubtful for them. We can and must love others and yet address the good and bad in their behavior.

ACKNOWLEDGEMENTS

I am deeply thankful for those who have not only been essential in the creation of this book, but to all who have been a part of my journey, especially those who taught me to address matters, and those who have endured with me as I (mostly) attempted to do so with wisdom, kindness, and empathy. I am continually reminded of how much room there is to improve.

INTRODUCTION

The purpose of this book is simple. To help you understand the why and how behind tackling issues in your life, particularly in relationships, with a focus on handling confrontation.

You will find the start of this book identifying confrontation, and giving it a workable definition, as well as hopefully helping you put it in proper perspective.

Next, we will discuss why engaging in healthy confrontation is beneficial for all of us, and the perils of avoiding confrontation at all costs.

Following this we will look at some pattern behaviors that we can hopefully identify in ourselves and others. We will gain insight into how these behaviors work and sustain themselves.

Since we have opened a can of worms by looking at challenging behavior patterns and stress responses, we need to make a final thrust into the dirt to discover what drives us, makes us tick, and how can we truly become better as individuals. The spillover effect here is that every area of our life is better when we deal with our most profound beliefs about self.

Now, what you are waiting for, wanting most, and hopefully will use time and time again; the process of preparing and executing a conversation where you must confront someone. This chapter contains the blueprint for a compassionate and understanding attempt at resolving issues.

To cement this process, we lay out additional strategies that can help us in our quest to have excellent communication.

Finally, we close with motivation and encouragement for the journey, defining the future for our lives after we leap into an attitude that says, "I can deal with my issues head-on without procrastinating."

WHAT THIS BOOK WILL DO FOR YOU

In every chapter of this book you will find reasons, ways, and examples that will enable you to make your life better by dealing with the important issues you are facing.

1

WHAT IS CONFRONTATION?

"Dealt with it!" she said as she looked me square in the eye. "If you don't like the way that things are, then do something about it. You keep complaining and acting like things are supposed to fix themselves. The people you work with, your boss, your friends, your health, the finances. You are the one putting up with it, and your complaining about it isn't helping. Why don't you just speak up for yourself and say something to them? Why don't you do something?"

Maybe parts of this conversation sound familiar to you and perhaps not. At some point, we have all been challenged by people and problems in our life. The question is: how did we choose to respond? Did we step up and deal with it? Or did we just let it be?

Let me tell you about a friend of mine. Aaron is a man who refuses to deal with anything in his life. He prefers to let things be instead of risking the discomfort of change, the possibility of rejection, or the opportunity for failure. He refuses to change his eating and lack of exercise and is therefore in a state of poor health. There is no doubt that his health is affecting every other area of his life as well. Poor health and poor body image often translate into having less energy, feeling less secure, being looked over for promotions at work, crankiness and a host of issues. This inability to confront others has a significant impact on how he and his wife are raising their children. The children lack discipline and are suffering because of it. Unable to enforce something as simple as a bedtime means that they stay up late - until the parents go to bed. As a result, they can't focus when at school, so although bright, their performance suffers. The same lack of discipline around diet also creates health issues for the children. Eating pizza and macaroni and cheese means bowel issues and childhood obesity. For there to be genuine respect in the marriage, there must be a level of communication. How do you respect someone who cannot just speak up? So like everyone else, his wife walks all over him and also lives an undisciplined life - overspending, escaping as often as possible, and neglecting the needs of the family. Young children need attention and structure to grow holistically. In the end, everyone in the entire family experiences various levels of dysfunction.

Maybe you think that confrontation is unpleasant and ugly? The truth is that we often know what it is we need to face but wish to avoid.[1] As we can see above, avoidance has consequences, and that is why it is crucial to address issues quickly.

Confrontation isn't limited to verbal disagreements. It also means dealing with things that matter. Confrontation makes way for positive change and improvement because it initiates a conversion from one state of being to another by addressing the things that need to change.

Confrontation: the act of confronting: the state of being confronted: as a: a face-to-face meeting b: the clashing of forces or ideas: conflict

Confront (simple definition)
: to oppose or challenge (someone) especially in a direct and forceful way
: to directly question the action or authority of (someone)
: to deal with (something, such as a problem or danger); especially: to deal with (something) in an honest and direct way
*Courtesy of Merriam Webster

AS YOU WILL LEARN THROUGHOUT THIS BOOK, CONFRONTATION

Is to face or deal with something head-on.
Is often done in an attempt to preserve a relationship.
Need not involve fear, angry emotions and be unbearable.
Should not be avoided in most cases.

Confrontation is essential for positive change in life. It is key to problem resolution, as well as maintaining healthy relationships. It means to address what needs to be addressed directly.

Confrontation is a vital part of preserving relationships. Most of our issues involve relationships with other people. Sometimes we lose relationships with others because we can't seem to resolve our differences for one reason or another. Delaying tough conversations can often lead to tragic outcomes in familial situations like divorce and family feuds. At work, the outcomes may manifest as fractured business partnerships and costly lawsuits. If we don't attempt to work it out, how can we find a solution?

We can't advance, succeed, or grow without confrontation. Engaging in productive and compassionate discourse paves the way for the diversity of thought, developing healthy boundaries, arriving at new, innovative approaches, better decision-making, and challenging the status quo, all of which are essential if we want to thrive in our lives and work.

COMMON MYTHS AND PITFALLS ABOUT CONFRONTATION

There are many untrue things people believe that keep them from confronting anyone or anything, along with false ideas of how it has to look and feel.

Hoping it just "works out" magically*. This is a big one. The idea that somehow everything will work out all by itself, or by us doing nothing. Typically nothing is further from the truth. Usually, things get worse when we do nothing. James is a boss I know who refuses to correct or fire bad employees in hopes that they will eventually leave if he ignores them. He alternatively suggests that further training will help but without considering the possibility that the problem employee doesn't have the aptitude or fit for the job. Anything is a better alternative to him disciplining or firing someone. Meanwhile, he also ignores the cost of training in lost revenue, and time demands on the organization. The results are frustrating to good employees who do their jobs, and costly to the business.

How about cancer? Naturally, no one thinks that doing nothing about it is a good idea because it spreads, sometimes quickly. Doing nothing means it could grow to the point that treatment will not do much good. Bullies? Until you expose or stand up to a bully, you will continue to be on the receiving end of abusive domination. Doing nothing is not going to help. With the millions of examples we could cite, it clear to see that hoping that problems solve themselves is merely "wishful thinking."

Confrontation is painful and for type A personalities. This idea is often based off of prior negative experiences with aggressive individuals but is also not true. Unfortunately, many people think that going off on others is cool, justified, or acceptable. Entire regions and cities are known for overly direct and at times coarse forms of interaction.[2] Today's Twitter wars and Facebook debates only exacerbate the ability of people to be rude and compassionless.[3] Also called emotional hijacking, this kind of aggressive behavior looks like one person yelling, debasing, demeaning, and often cursing out another. No one would enjoy being on the receiving end of that, and who wants to be that person doing the giving part? That, however, is not what confrontation is. That is purely immature and uncontrolled behavior that was never corrected. Perhaps it was learned from others. Regardless, there is a better way to get your point across. An approach that doesn't leave others scarred and humiliated.

Confrontation doesn't have to be painful, forceful, unpleasant, or aggressive. In fact, parents, counselors, psychologists, chaplains, first responders, coaches, and diplomats are a few examples of careers where one must be able to address challenging situations in a peaceful and controlled manner. Anyone who has to deal with other people will need to learn to confront if they wish to excel in life. Think of the police officer or counselor who talks down a suicidal person, negotiates a hostage release, or clergy that helps others move on after a terrible loss. All of these people are community leaders who must address a difficult situation without losing patience or control. All of these professionals realize that their ability to keep control over their emotions can dramatically increase their effectiveness in helping others and improving lives. We could call these people role models.

It's best to "keep the peace." Maybe you have heard this one before? The problem with this statement is that peace isn't always synonymous with quiet. Peace is the absence of conflict, while quiet is the absence of noise. Conflicts are enforced by silence and dispelled through dialog. Keeping quiet often perpetuates disputes that will only be resolved by talking. Those who favor not speaking up in favor of keeping the peace, most often do so because they fear the outcome of speaking up may be much worse. Those who cling to this philosophy as a mantra might shudder at the very thought of a verbal confrontation. Regardless of the cost, most people will do anything to avoid having to confront someone or something. While this seems logical on one side, in reality, this doesn't create peace but instead shifts conflicts inwards. Secret loathing, despising can take root and build up. Many people today are just unaware of how their lives are run and limited by fear. Living in fear is not peace, is it? An example of this: fearing that the confrontation will become an out of control traumatic encounter as previously mentioned. The fear is based on the belief that the outcome of confronting or speaking up will be worse than putting up with the person's behavior or circumstance they are facing. Perhaps they have been abandoned or rejected by others in the past and fear that after the conversation this person will reject them. Maybe this is a workplace issue, and they fear that they could lose their job for speaking up. Or perhaps they fear that no matter how they try to say what is on their mind that they will be perceived as that aggressive and attacking person they can't stand. All of these fears (and others) can keep us in the bondage of living in silence. This is a kind of slavery where our thoughts, feelings, rights, and self-expression are tied up and suppressed. As a result, we are held captive. It is fear like this that dupes us into submission, cowardice, and subjugation. As individuals, we become paralyzed by fear, and cannot move forward in life.

Relationship, career, you name it. All are going nowhere. Often these fears are unfounded or wildly exaggerated. Even if there is a chance that we will face new issues by bringing out our feelings and letting the truth come to the surface, there is something else we need to consider: speaking up may ultimately help those we are afraid of offending, inciting or arousing. At the very least, we cannot address our feelings if we hide them. We may have no reason to know if our assertions are correct if we don't communicate. Why be a prisoner?

A police officer can't be afraid to confront a criminal because keeping the peace also means facing the disorderly and unlawful. There is no peace without order. Order requires confronting disorder. These simple truths tell us that what we need is to stop trying to find the best way to avoid what is difficult, but rather the best way to simplify or handle what's difficult.

You can't avoid every issue. You can't eliminate the existence of problems - they are a part of life. You can only choose to change the way you handle them. You can change the way you deal with people, problems and you can even change your viewpoint.

Confrontation is just too "difficult." You can go ahead and insert your word of choice here; awkward, complicated, or painful. How difficult it is to do something is often a matter of perspective, or viewpoint, as well as ability. To lift 100 pounds may be nearly impossible for one person, and yet a piece of cake for another. To solve a math problem could be difficult for one person, and easy for another. The difference is not only in natural ability, but training, learning, and conditioning. Quite often, people fail to attempt things because they perceive their capacity less than the difficulty of the task. Many times I have witnessed people do something they thought that they could not and afterward proclaim,

"Wow, that was easier than I thought." It is the same with confrontation. It is easier to do than you realize.

No one learns to ride a bike without a fall. Many will skin a knee. The secret is to get back up and on the bicycle. Success often means being undeterred from the mistakes and mishaps that will happen when learning and improving skills.

Can't you teach an old dog new tricks?
No one is too old to learn. Once thought not to be true, numerous studies have confirmed that intelligence can be increased later in life.[4] Evidence abounds that proves that everyone (yes, that includes you) can change, regardless of age or other factors.

You Cannot Change What You Refuse To Confront

"I want a divorce," she said. Jim's heart wrenched, his throat went dry as he tried to mumble a rejection. "No, I mean it. I can't do this anymore." Here they were, finally out on a date, and "this is what I am hearing?" Jim thought. Everything in him went into defense mode, and as the comments kept coming, both anger and despair grew inside of him. *More than ever this was the moment that he needed not to explode or withdraw, but listen and communicate.*

Maybe you know a Jim - I think I know several. Jim doesn't do well with being confronted.

Maybe you know someone like Jim's wife? Try as she might to get through, it seems that either no one is listening or that she may get her head chopped off as the profanity-laden name-calling and attacks come at her. She just wished she knew how to get her message to her husband so that they could make this thing work. The truth of the matter is that most of the time Jane was not forthright and had let her husband think that things were beautiful until she could no longer stand it. *What if there was a better way, a way to bring some changes in this marriage?*

Confrontation Makes Way For Positive Change

You cannot change what you refuse to confront. Maybe there are some situations that you would like to see change? Perhaps you are fed up with being fed up? Have you ever felt like life is passing you by? Maybe you think that everyone else has it easier than you. How would you like to turn the tables? Stop hiding what you think? Take control of your destiny? Find a way to fix the mistakes of the past - a way to speak up and speak out without fear? *Are you ready to quit playing it safe?*

Each person has a unique promise, value, and voice. All too often these things are hidden, unrecognized, and silenced. Maybe it's time that you found your voice, understood your promise and recognized your value?

I want to show you how to communicate your way through the barriers that block your progress and happiness, so that you can tackle your problems head-on, and take charge of your life and situation.

Now, let's be clear: You can't change how old you are, where you grew up, and the events and circumstances of your past. You can't necessarily determine what kind of unexpected life events or situations you may face today or tomorrow.

You can, however, determine how you will respond, what kind of person you will be, what you will be known for and what path you are charting. At any time we choose, we can start planning and working towards our goals. You can harness the innate, God-given power of choice, the forces of hope, love, faith, and forgiveness to reconcile past hurts, believe in yourself and your future, and to build a bridge into your destiny.

This book is a starting place. It is the necessary first step, perhaps, to believe that things can change for you. Believe that you can change, and you will be able to change things!

Today is your day to begin a new chapter in your life. It is your day to find the way, the strength, and the will to overcome disappointment and regret. Let's begin this journey together. To start, we must understand some truths that will empower you to overcome your current limitations.

Confrontation Means Telling The Truth

Confrontation involves *digging up the truth*. Sometimes it is what we want out of life and our desires that we don't communicate, other times it is taking a stand against what we don't want. Truth is essential to the idea of confrontation because being truthful requires us to recognize the responsibility we have for our actions and inactions. Truth can also refer to something that is immutable, secure, reliable, inherent. In this sense, we are speaking about timeless principles. These kinds of truth are a part of this book. These laws become a foundation for building our lives. Commonly accepted truths are known as principles or first things. If we are going to learn to change our lives and deal with others, we must be honest with them and ourselves. We also need to say what we mean and *mean what we say*. We need to tell the truth. *What else?* We can't ignore the consequences of our behavior. When we pretend that our actions don't have any effect, we are deceiving ourselves.

Pretending that gravity is not real when jumping free fall from altitude is not a wise decision. Repeatedly stating that there is no such thing as gravity will not cause you to escape the repercussions of such a choice.

Ignoring principles of responsibility, communication, forgiveness, trust, honesty, and diligence will not allow you to escape their consequences.

All communication has the potential to add value. "Think before you speak" is something that was once taught in school. It meant taking into consideration how *what* you

12

say will make others feel, and what it will convey about you. We should always think about the outcome we want before we speak or write.

Learning to say "No."

Another reason we need to speak up is to set boundaries with the people in our lives. "Setting boundaries" means being able to say "no" to people. Your success in life depends on both what you say "yes" to and those to which you say "no". Often, saying "no" is the more important choice. Save your energy for what matters. There is a limit to the amount of brainpower, time, and energy you can use in a single day. You can only live each day once. You can spend the same dollar only once; if you waste it, you can't get it back. Time is precious.

Grace was exhausted. Her clothes needed ironing, she needed to go grocery shopping, and yet there she was again, about to walk out of the office after another long after-hours workday when she stopped in observance of the vibration in her purse. It was her supervisor on the cell phone - she broke a little on the inside because she knew what was coming. It was always something. Something else that he needed to be done. Something important. Something that kept her from getting back to normal - getting caught up. The urgent thing changed often, but the pattern was always the same. "Grace, I hate to ask, but would you be able to see this through today or tonight? I promise we will make this one up to you."

Empty words, but Grace said to herself, "I'm going out of my way to be a good sport. These are good people."

The problem was not only at work with her boss. It was also her niece, her neighbor, and her incarcerated brother who were always adding the requests. Candy and muffins helped her cope with the pressure and despair but added to the health issues that she already had as a person with type 2 diabetes. Grace's problem wasn't her evil boss and demanding inner circle, it was her "heart of gold." She couldn't say no to anyone. While some people are dealing with aggressive bullying, it didn't take all that much to get Grace to do what you want - you only had to ask. *She never said no.*

> *When you allow others to determine the quality*
> *of your life, you will always be miserable.*

Speaking up to create and enforce some personal boundaries will prevent your life from being run by the demands of others. *When you allow others to determine the quality of your life, you will always be miserable.* It will fall short of your dreams when you let others put you into the box they think suits you. That box, and subsequently your life, will end up being too small. Don't let others determine how far you should go, how big your world should be, and how you should spend your time.

Now, part of this will come down to you addressing your convictions so that you can make sound decisions in your life. Personal convictions are beliefs about what is the right course of action. Although we usually know what is the right thing to do, doing it often seems challenging for several reasons. We find conflict with sound decision making because of emotions and fears. Sources of conflict in our life don't usually come entirely from the present circumstances, but often these have arisen due to:

past hurts
past failures
personal injustices
lack of attention to feelings
lack of addressing problems

Confrontation becomes necessary when we have a situation or person that we don't want to face or deal with directly. As you can see in this list above, all of these issues require some form of (possibly uncomfortable) confrontation to resolve.

Confrontation is an attempt to preserve a relationship.

Confront those that you value.

Confrontation shows that you not only care about yourself but that you care about others. Once while in my gym, I remember watching a group of guys I knew performing an exercise known as the squat. While there are several variations of the squat, the goal is to lower your body by sitting back and bending your knees. One of these guys was leaning forward way too far and moving all of the weight with his back - he looked like a chicken pecking at the floor while only slightly bending his knees. Because he was using quite a bit of weight and straining hard, I was shocked that his companions weren't even saying anything. I walked right up (as I knew these guys) and told him, "these guys aren't your friends because what you are doing right there is dangerous." I asked him for his phone and then took a quick video while he attempted to do the exercise again. When he saw what he was doing, he was shocked! He thanked me, and I made the point to his friends that they should be looking out for him. Often, looking out for someone means interjecting, interrupting, or confronting.

Confronting others is (often) a moral responsibility.

There are many situations where we have a clear and direct responsibility to tell someone if they are doing something wrong. Perhaps what they are doing is dangerous, illegal, careless, or just plain ignorant. Maybe they don't know any better, or they know, but they think it's inconsequential, or they make excuses for their behavior.

Wise men of ancient times once instructed the people by saying, "tell your brother his fault." They said, "Don't gossip, defraud or slander. When you do this, you ruin others' lives, and this is proof that you hate others. Instead of hating the one you are mad at, go and tell them you are upset and work things out. Telling them is proof that you are a person of love."

You have influence and the ability to make a difference. Every life matters and every word or action somehow will affect others. No man is an island. No man lives or dies entirely unto himself. We are all connected. In the movie, *Hugo*, the son of a mechanic and clockmaker struggles to find parts to fix his father's automaton - all that he has left after his father dies. He is befriended by a little girl in his pursuit and shares his discovery gleaned not only from his quest but daily observing the people below. He looks out at the world from the top of the clock tower and shares this wisdom with his only friend - there are no spare parts in life. Every person has a role to play, interdependent with other people. Every component is vital and essential and necessary. Just as the loss of one piece harms the machine, so the loss of one person has great significance. If you aren't playing your part - we all feel it. When you do contribute - we all feel it.

People Matter. You and I have a role to play. I wrote this book to help people live better lives, to improve families, companies, teams, nations.

If we were to think of people as individual parts of a body, that would help us to see that every one of us is crucial to the whole. Which part of your body would you like to be without? Even your fingernail is of vital importance. Trying to push a button or do basic tasks would be uncomfortable and more dangerous without it. It protects you. Many women use their fingernails as a form of expression. There are no spare parts. We must value ourselves and value others. Each person is unique. Each person has value. If your neighbor has value, then shouldn't you tell them if they are in danger?

As we begin to learn more about confrontation, I hope that you will come to see it as both strategic and tactical, direct and diplomatic. I hope that you will embrace the idea that taking action is necessary for positive change in your life and the lives of those around you. Confrontation can be a gateway to harmony, safety, and peace.

Dealing with issues in life is key to success and fulfillment. The Deal With It Philosophy is this: It is best to take care of things as they arise or as soon as we can. This prevents skeletons in the closet and a snowballing effect that occurs when issues grow in impact and importance due to neglect. There is no time like the present. The best time to do it is now.

2

WHY SHOULD WE CARE?
WHY SHOULD WE CONFRONT?

*Confrontation is a necessary and helpful part
of all interpersonal communication.*

WHY SHOULD WE CARE? WHY
SHOULD WE CONFRONT?

Imagine a life where you can always get things taken care of,
you set goals and achieve them. You are at peace with your
neighbors and coworkers and enjoy working with or on a
team or role that engages and depends on others. You are
not afraid to sit down and review your finances and plans
with your spouse, or fearful of bedtime with your kids. You
know that whatever it is, you always seem to work it out.

Additionally, you don't feel stressed, even though your day
and life are full of activities. Your health is something you
have a pretty good handle on because you see your doctor,

your trainer, and watch what you eat. At 45 you look and feel 35. Sound too good to be true? I am going to show you how to speak up for yourself. You will see not only how to do it, but what the results will be. I know what it means to have responsibility, pressure, and demands. After all, everyone has something they want or need from you, right? Let's flip the coin on this scenario for a minute, and then dive into specific reasons why dealing with it matters.

In this chapter, we are going to look at how our newly defined "Deal With It Philosophy" (DWIP), creates healthy relationships, healthy personal perspectives, and leads to a more meaningful and satisfying life. Before we do that, let's lay some groundwork as to the significance of interpersonal communication.

Why is it we sometimes don't get what we need or want from others? Or maybe it's the reverse, with others seeming to think you just don't "get" them? Humans must communicate to relate to one another. For us to know what others are feeling and let them know what we want, we need to talk. Communication defines relationships. What do I mean by that? The more communicating going on, the better your potential for a good relationship. The better the quality of the conversations, the better the relationship.

The goal of communication is shared understanding. We are social beings. We not only need others, but we also cannot exist without others.[1] There is a part of us that cannot be fulfilled or find joy without others. We gain a sense of our value from our interactions with others. It feels good to spend time with Bae, Boo, Baby, Hubby, Wife, or whoever.

20

You undoubtedly were created to love and to be loved. Understanding love brings clarity to a part of the human existence. *Reconciling the difficulties and complexities of love, friendship, and companionship are essential tasks of human life and society.* We are a part of one another - we are a single race unified in our pursuit of some expression. This expression is what humanity has struggled continually to grasp throughout the ages. Thought and a thirst for *why* are both evidence of a *why*.

So with all this mushy love and feel good time spent together, why do we have so many issues and problems? My Jewish uncle used to say, "where you have two Jews, you have three arguments." The idea has nothing to do with being Jewish, but rather the experience of not being able to agree with others.[2] When two people come together for a conversation, we have two unique brains, minds, and individual perspectives coming together, and quite often they collide. There may be a clash over the differences of view. Of course, we must communicate in ways that allow others to gain some insight into our thoughts and viewpoints and be able to disagree without going berserk.

Communication means to be united by what we share (rather than divided). We speak and act to share our feelings, preferences, desires. We don't just make our thoughts known; we make ourselves known. Others will feel loved (or at least liked) by perceiving that you understand and value them. To love someone then is to share in that person - bringing an understanding of their identity into your life. Getting to know someone requires spending enough time with them so that you can develop (in your mind) who they are. This ability to relate to one another is the goal of communication of all kinds.

Media profiles have become problematic today because reading about someone can create a false idea of who that person is. With no personal experience, you may not have a genuine picture of that person. Knowing about someone and knowing someone are not the same thing.

Most of our communication problems stem from the way we think and perceive ourselves and the world, and these thought patterns both affect and are affected by how others treat us.[3] We can't change the latter but we can the former. Our relationships and experiences have shaped us, but that doesn't mean that we should let them define us.

There are some excellent reasons why we should deal with the issues (and people) in our life. Let's explore.

Why Should We Confront?

Reason #1 - Your Health Matters

Health - Do not let the sun go down on your wrath

Ever have trouble sleeping at night because of some exchange or something that happened during the day? Maybe it was something you said or did that wasn't right. Perhaps it was something your boss or a colleague said to you. Perhaps you were stood up, lied to, treated poorly or just ignored.

Need to escape the day and find yourself reaching for alcohol, substances or unhealthy relationships?
Need to escape nearly every day because work is just "killing you"?
Are you living for the weekend, vacations, or some other momentary escape?

While a "yes" might fit you in with millions of people, it's also a clue that you need to make changes. Perhaps it's not the way your day goes, but one, two or more specific people that are the problem? Or maybe you are having an issue with yourself? Yes, it is possible that you are continually upset with yourself at how you handled or didn't handle a particular situation, what you said or didn't say.

Do you ever find yourself fretting about work or family exchanges/drama? Replaying them continually and unable to talk or think about anything else?

This kind of fixation has negative impacts on your physical, emotional, and social health.[4] Not only the actions, but the feelings and thoughts themselves are stress-causing factors that diminish the quality of life. Your loss of peace, joy, focus, and satisfaction in life not only robs you but robs others around you (friends, family, employers) of the true you.

We now know that almost all major diseases (heart disease, cancer, hypertension) are mainly stress related. Relational issues are killing people both directly through emotional stress and indirectly through how many people attempt to deal with stress. While there are several positive ways to deal with stress such as:

prayer
exercise[5]
meditation
hot baths
art and other hobbies

there are also most often many other ways people deal with stress such as:

binge eating
staying out and up late
prescription drugs
alcohol and substances from cigarettes to illegal drugs
loose living

These negative behaviors are all efforts to distract or find comfort for the moment, but all will destroy your life physically, emotionally, mentally, socially and spiritually.

~ People Issues ~

It is our responsibility to make our thoughts and emotions known to others.

We all know people that are difficult to talk to. In fact, there is pretty much no way to avoid encountering them at some point in life. They could just be having a bad day, or they could be a certified bully. Maybe they are verbally assaulting you to get their way or using sarcastic insinuations to demean you. Perhaps they assemble a coup against anyone who doesn't go their way. Or it could be that they take advantage of you by pressuring you to do something that you shouldn't. Perhaps you think that you are being nice by going along, even when you know you will regret it later? There is a high price to be paid for failing to stand up for yourself. It isn't so much their fault for sucking you dry, as much as it might be yours. Remember how Grace was always caving to her boss? It was in her power to stop doing that at any time. She merely had to say "No." Grace had become her own worst enemy. Her fear of the consequences had caused her to be everyone's servant.

Understanding the potential emotional and physical ramifications of being a so-called "nice guy."

There is a real difference between genuinely being kind or flexible (a "nice guy"), and just being afraid to speak your mind. If we don't speak our minds and as a result are upset with others because it seems they don't "respect us enough to ask our opinion," we are living with unrealistic expectations. Regardless of whether they were thinking of you or not, there may be a reason for their behavior, even if that reason is poor communication skill on their part. We need to recognize that it is our responsibility to make our thoughts and emotions known to others. People don't read minds, and truthfully many people are not all that advanced when it comes to interpreting the *nonverbal expressions* of others. The surprising result: We often fail to understand others. We judge people for not asking us our thoughts and yet ignore the fact that we haven't asked why they haven't asked us. Our non-communication makes it impossible for us to know what factors are influencing their behavior.

Neither should we blame others for being ignorant of our situation or point of view if we haven't attempted to make them understand. Two people with dysfunctional communication skills won't make solid contact unless one steps out of their pattern.

The fear of speaking up creates a pattern of frustration and anger, often leading to resentment or outbursts of some kind.[6] By keeping these conflicts alive internally, we also put unnecessary stress on ourselves.

What happens when we tolerate this pattern of fear, frustration, and anger? Stress on the body.

Fear, frustration, anxiety, and anger result in undue stress on our bodies. Along with physical stress, these destructive emotions release a hormone called cortisol. This hormone has many adverse effects and produces proteins that can shrink the brain.[7]

Here are a few of the things cortisol affects:

- Blood sugar (glucose) levels
- Fat, protein and carbohydrate metabolism to maintain blood glucose (gluconeogenesis)
- Immune responses
- Anti-inflammatory actions
- Blood pressure
- Heart and blood vessel tone and contraction

- Central nervous system activation

Canadian Clinician Dr. James Wilson notes:

While it is vital to health for the adrenals to secrete cortisol in response to stress, it is also vital that bodily functions and cortisol levels return to normal following a stressful event. Unfortunately, in our current high-stress culture, the stress response is activated so often that the body does not always have a chance to return to normal. This pattern leads to health problems.[8]

Recent studies from Yale illustrate how stress can shrink your brain. The parts of your brain that help you think through and make important decisions are at risk, as well as areas that affect motivation. The neurons and their dendrites, (the structures that connect neurons and allow the parts of your brain to send messages and process thought, or recall memories) can atrophy from stress. This phenomenon has been observed specifically in the prefrontal cortex (PFC), a part of the brain responsible for metabolism, glucose, emotional processing, and problem-solving. The striatum, another part of the brain that processes motivation and gratification, can also be affected, impacting your happiness. Brain shrinkage corresponds with a loss of memory function, difficulty thinking, or synthesis of information. The frontal cortex can become deteriorated, including areas responsible for reasoning, planning, memory, and problem-solving.[9]

These are serious consequences that we need to consider carefully. Again, we now know that a primary cause of all fatal disease is stress. Quality of life is more than things or status. Quality of life is first and foremost peace of mind. We must find a way to reduce, prevent, and deal with stress, including the stressors that arise from inadequate or missed (lack of) communication.

The adage ascribed to Eleanor Roosevelt declares, "No one can make you feel inferior without your consent." But the same should be true for anger and frustration: No one can make you upset without your permission.

Now, how is that possible? Isn't getting upset a natural reaction?

While getting upset is perhaps a typical reaction, it is also a controllable action. We can choose not to get upset, to keep our emotions in check and be a person of peace.[10] Later in this book, we will learn strategies to do just this.

Why Should We Confront?

Reason #2 - Your Voice Matters

You may need to speak up because the issue doesn't go away or won't get resolved otherwise. Avoiding those you live and work with is not an option. Remember, it's a small world, after all. You will still have to deal with the person, and avoiding them will make life more difficult and exhausting. The reality is that you should be confident enough to step up and work it out. Something else to consider: lousy news doesn't improve with time. Concealing will only make the implications of the bad behavior worse (no matter who is at fault). If the other person knows that you were holding out on them, they may have some resentment against you when they find out. Conversely, if you are having an issue with them, you may begin to consciously or unconsciously resent them until you deal with it, *face to face*. This is because the way we feel about others eventually (if not immediately) will always affect how we treat them. Believing anything else is pure deception and quite frankly, more work than resolving the situation.

Building a healthy relationship requires honesty and that often means that there will be difficulty that tests the relationship as we are honest about disappointments and disagreements. Spouses must work through the first fight if they are going to work through their marriage. Since we are all unique in our opinions, all relationships that last (no matter the level of intimacy) will require working through differences.

Confront when the relationship matters, (*hint*: almost always). The more valuable, the more critical it is to confront issues that arise. Continually going to someone over every little thing can become a nagging and harping annoyance that leads to more stress and constant strife. On the other hand, working through a conflict can build stronger relationships.[11] What we will deal with in Chapter 5 is how to best frame the conversation to build trust and respect.

Your Reputation Matters.

Want others to take you seriously? Say what you mean, and mean what you say. Stick to your guns and don't be ashamed to have an opinion. "Boy, it sure would feel good to tell them how I feel." We say that, and we think of the outcome, but what if you can have your cake and eat it too? What if you tell them how you feel in a way that doesn't destroy your reputation but builds it? What if you were known as a "straight shooter," honest, and the person that people can come to for advice because they respect how you handle yourself? You are a bridge builder and not a bully. You find a way to mediate disputes and settle disagreements. A sort of communication super-hero? *Pull up your pants, Mighty Mouse, because, with a little help, you got this.* People will respect you more for being forthright, and that respect is magnified by the degree to which you can do it with class.

Why Should We Confront?

Reason #3 - To Help Others Grow

It is sometimes impossible to help others without being direct or correcting them. Should a parent or a teacher not correct their children or students? That would be preposterous. Most problems just aren't solved by being ignored. To pretend that we are somehow doing the right thing by not showing others where they can learn, improve, or examine themselves is deception. We can pretend that letting others always have their way is the best course of action and even noble, but if that means we enable others to live in dysfunction and shirk their responsibility, we are preventing them from growing (and we deny a truth about humanity). There is a word for someone who always gives in to the demands of others even when it's not in the best interest of either party: a pushover.

Children often use tactics to avoid punishments from their parents such as crying, and a soft parent may refuse to correct a child. Refusing to raise our children is extremely dangerous. Failure to impose consequences for improper actions gives children a deceived view of reality. They will be met with harsher judgment in the outside world and must be prepared to respect laws, rules, and authority. Otherwise, they may end up in the worst of circumstances.

The same principle is true for any teacher of a craft. A music or dance instructor will critique the slightest imperfections in pose, form, timing, or training. It takes discipline to develop mastery. Without someone who can push you to improve, there will be no mastery.

The same is true in psychology. Some people are always allowing others to push them around. Their lack of backbone needs to be called out, while those doing the pushing should be told to back down.

Let me give you another example of how confronting a person about their situation can lead them to face the people and the issues in their life.

Marcus was a brilliant man, financially successful, and with some signs of social success. Despite this, he was plagued with emotional and physical health issues and had a hard time developing relationships with others. Furthermore, he was also unable to take criticism of any kind and had no contact with any of his extended family. While having a conversation over lunch, we somehow got onto the topic of fatherlessness and how it impacts children. Little did I know, his father abandoned him as an infant.

As the conversation progressed, I related the story of David, a client of mine whose father also left the house when he was young. It had impacted his self-esteem, which in turn affected every other area of his life. His ability to communicate, relate, find acceptance, advance vocationally, all seemed to be held back. Even his ability to stick to a diet and exercise routine. When we finally convinced him to track down and talk to his father, he was extremely nervous. In the end, he ambushed his dad by just showing up at his house. Although the first meeting was awkward - over time they began to meet and talk. As a result of these meetings, David had an important realization. All of his life he thought that his father left them because he didn't love them enough to stay. He had internalized this belief, translating it into a sense of worthlessness. It was this low self-worth or lack of self-love that had prevented him from growing in any way. After all, if you are no good, why even try to do the things that others do? However it happened, his father told him that he had been abandoned by his father as well. Also having a family, he felt that he was no good, and out of his fear and personal issues he left. Eventually, David's father told him "I ran away because there was something wrong with me. I didn't deserve you. There was nothing wrong with you." As you can imagine, this new information shifted David's conclusions about the events and his beliefs. In turn, he no longer had to accept his negative feelings about himself. The change in his behavior was radically positive. He began to take better care of himself; his posture changed, he no longer had issues looking people in the eye. He went back to school, stopped jumping from place to place, started a business, and got married. This story is just one case that shows us how anyone can change.

As I relayed this story to Marcus, he began to realize that many problems in his life centered around this very issue. He asked if we could speak more about this and realized he had to find some way to address it - but how? The simple answer was to confront his birth father, who had abandoned him and his mother. Only through a confrontation could the emotions and hurt be dealt with and would there be a chance for reconciliation. As he talked it through, he realized that it was necessary, but with so many unknowns and hurts, he was not sure if he could. Marcus decided to start with a baby step. First, he told his wife about the issue and how he felt. In 15 years of marriage, they had never talked about his father in depth at all. Second, they identified a related incident with his half-sister that he felt he needed to resolve. The insult that caused the rift had been bothering him and his wife for years. Marcus decided to start by calling her and apologizing. It was so out of character for him to reach out to his family, that when Marcus had to text another relative for his half-sister's phone number, they immediately thought he might be dying. After making the call, apologizing, and reconciling with this sibling, he felt a kind of relief that he had never experienced. "*Like a weight being lifted.*" It is this kind of confrontation that can heal families and bring unity among the fragmented. Real stories like Marcus' show us how simple it can be to improve the quality of our lives. As we begin to realize the impact of our actions on others and realize that we care about how we treat them, that is true love at work. Everyone around us benefits when we do the right thing.

Today, Marcus has reunited with his estranged birth father (and much of his family), finding healing for the painful wounds of rejection, betrayal, and abandonment. His kids are thrilled at having a grandfather and finding joy with their cousins. He has improved his marriage and learned how to receive feedback a little better. Marcus learned that the truth might hurt a little, but it is worth it to embrace the difficulty of change and confrontation, because of the healing that it can bring.

It is when we show others how they can change that we create opportunities for change in their life. As they choose to deal with it, they introduce change.

I love the story of the grandfather walking the beach with his grandson. Every step or two the grandfather would reach down, pick up a sand dollar and throw it out to sea. He'd take a couple more steps, pick up another one and throw it out, and another one, and finally the grandson said, "Granddaddy, what are you doing?" And the grandfather said, "Son, these sand dollars are living organisms. If I don't throw them out to sea, they'll die in the hot sun. They've been washed ashore by the tide." The grandson said, "But, Granddaddy, there are thousands of them. What possible difference can it make?" And the grandfather reached down, picked up another one, threw it out to sea and said, "To this one, it makes all the difference in the world." [12]

The proof that you love someone is the willingness to correct them.

I had to confront the guy in the gym about his form for him to correct it. I confronted Marcus' belief that nothing would change by forgiving his father. A coach must confront you to tell what you are doing wrong and how to correct it. My high school cross country coach confronted my bad attitude about running extra laps at the end of a practice. Correction is showing someone the right way to do something. It is partly in taking the risk of offending someone that our real motives are revealed. When we reach out and confront someone with the aim of helping (despite a personal cost or risk), we can reveal true love. *Love is what you do for another out of a desire to see their good, or benefit.* It is the aim of benefitting another that is love in essence or spirit. *It is the act of serving to another's benefit that is the demonstration of love or love in action.* That being said, love also uses discretion, and that means often speaking in a way that is sensitive to the individual's feelings and the situation. We don't want to embarrass or make a spectacle of someone's issue.

Why Should We Confront?

Reason #4 - Improve the World

As you turn your focus outward (toward helping and loving others), you will also find greater health inward (loving and helping yourself). The motivation for self-efficacy becomes a legacy of leadership, and by that, I mean serving others.

35

Nearly everyone is familiar with the golden rule: Do unto others as you would like them to do unto you.[13] The principle here is caring for others. It means putting their best interest in mind. Their best interest doesn't necessarily mean what feels comfortable to them. The implications of this principle (caring for others) are massive, with the potential to impact all aspects of society.

This rule also means standing up for others when necessary as well as living decently, orderly, and truthfully. It (most of the time) also means being a rule follower. When we break the rules, we lose our ability to enforce rules.

The reality is that we need *everyday heroes*. People who live daily with great character and moral courage. You don't have to be famous to champion a cause or to become one of these *everyday heroes*. You only need to do what is right in your daily life. By listening to conscience, everyday heroes make the world a better place. You can start by defining and understanding your values and living by them daily.

"Every time we turn our heads the other way when we see the law flouted, when we tolerate what we know to be wrong, when we close our eyes and ears to the corrupt because we are too busy or too frightened, when we fail to speak up and speak out, we strike a blow against freedom and decency and justice."

— Robert F. Kennedy

"Let no one be discouraged by the belief there is nothing one person can do against the enormous array of the world's ills, misery, ignorance, and violence. Few will have the greatness to

bend history, but each of us can work to change a small portion of events. And in the total of all those acts will be written the history of a generation."

— Robert F. Kennedy

When we fail to confront those who defy established valuable morals and principles, we lose as a society. Author Ed Cole put it this way: "If you accept someone else's philosophy that is merely a rationalization to justify their failure, then you accept their failure."[14]

It is impossible to be a person of integrity and avoid confrontation in life. Integrity requires that we do what's right because it's right. We tell the truth because it's the right thing to do. We stand up for what we believe in because we believe in it.

Why Should We Confront?

Reason #5 - Your Money is on the Line

Your ability to confront people, perspectives, and problems have significant influence over your financial outcomes. Money? Yes, absolutely.

Let's start with divorce, for instance. The average divorce costs about $20,000 in fees alone. There are also costs associated with loss of work time, reduced productivity, and possible alimony payments. Opportunity costs for investments or business owners are also often lost. Additionally, consider the lost financial benefit from either dual incomes or shared housing. Since home ownership has become how most people in the middle class can build wealth for retirement or their family, this is extremely concerning. The personal emotional and mental costs are beyond calculation, and it is not a positive financial event. This kind of tragedy scars individuals and their children, creates feelings of anger and bitterness in both, and often inferiority and insecurity in the children.

Aside from divorce, let's think about professional relationships. Most people do business with people they like. What does this have to do with confrontation, you might ask? Honestly, there are two things that I want you to consider. The first is that how you treat and speak to others can prevent or create problems and confrontation. Confrontations and difficulties most likely arise from unclear communication, lack of communication, or miscommunication. Miscommunication means that we say something, but it is not clear or specific. Lack of communication occurs when we don't speak up or reach out proactively to ask questions and share our mind. Miscommunication is when you spoke, but the message was not understood. You said A, and they heard B, just like the telephone game you may have played in school.

Confrontation is an opportunity to work through feelings and clear up any personal misconceptions you may have.

The second reason is that by being forthright and kind in your communication style, you will likely address most issues before they balloon into significant problems. In other words, we say what needs to be said with kindness and gentleness, and with understanding. It is easier to communicate with truthful people and preferable to deal with those we trust in business.

Since no relationship will last without some issues, being able to gain and keep business relationships will require learning to deal with problems when they arise, and before it is too late. Once there is an agreement, put things down in writing. Having contracts certainly helps in avoiding disputes.

You probably have worked hard enough to earn your money that you don't want to lose it over something that you can prevent, right? The truth is that you can likely improve your income if you learn how to speak up. Whether you work for someone or yourself, this is still true.

Mounting heaps of evidence show that those who can communicate best make the most.[16] Endless books on EQ or Emotional Quotient examine a different kind of intelligence that centers on emotional awareness.

Unions empower employees to confront business owners. Quarterly reviews and employee reviews are a chance for managers to confront and hear from subordinates. Peer reviews should be a place to introduce areas of uncertainty, potential conflicts and resolve differences and unspoken grievances that could tear teams apart, reduce efficiency, output, productivity, and ultimately revenues and profitability.

As a business leader, your team's ability to execute your vision is impacted by your ability to confront. When you communicate your vision to your team, you help bring focus, clarity, and motivation. A motivated and focused group will achieve more, and faster. That means more revenues, more profits. And what about a positive work culture? We hear so much about how culture trumps strategy. Honesty and open dialog help make a positive culture. Even companies with strong values often face internal conflicts that remain hidden and devalue their greatest asset, their people. People who are working well together exhibit creativity, drive, enthusiasm, and satisfaction.

The place you enjoy working at has people you enjoy working with. By learning to deal with issues such as conflicts, misunderstandings, and strong personalities, you can create an enjoyable workplace.

How do we make our workplace more enjoyable? We must make time for constructive criticism, feedback, and to talk about issues. As a manager, you must observe the rule of the internal SWOT, and examine the threats that can come from within the organization. We often don't know what is going on with people because we don't ask! The way to stay informed is by creating safe speaking environments and using discovery questions to learn what people are thinking.

Now it's true that people do not always share even when asked, and as mentioned, there are some excellent reasons why people might not want to expose themselves. There are good ways to make people feel comfortable and share. Some tips on how to do this will be outlined later in this book.

When you allow others to speak, you enable them to resolve the situation on their own. Have you ever been sharing with someone and said, "Now I realize how silly that sounds," or "I see how obvious the answer is." Just by talking about feelings or issues we may realize what we could not see before. Just by hearing it they may suddenly realize how simple the answer (or how silly their perspective) is. It isn't just voicing something, but subsequently hearing it, that triggers a review by the mind and heart and can cause an internal reckoning to take place. You can sometimes point out to someone what they have said - "what I just heard you say was" to help them realize and address their thoughts.

The reason we should confront others is to resolve the issues and conflicts we have with them. Learning to do this well directly impacts your business and intimate relationships.

Why Should We Confront?

Reason #6 - Peace is Priceless

Your emotional health matters. By taking the opportunity to work through disagreement and de-escalate the conflict in the workplace, home, or shared space, we not only solve those issues, but we prevent a whole host of other problems. Although we have spoken about physical (and mental) health, let's take a look at this from the perspective of emotional health. Grace was frazzled. Her inability to speak up, say no, confront her boss, and break the cycle had driven her into a deep depression. She felt captive, defeated, and even hopeless. Conflicted about doing what she thought was right (saying yes all the time) and doing what she needed to do for herself (putting a priority on taking care of herself), she had lost her sense of inner peace. Maybe you can relate? Is there a situation that seems as though you can't do anything about it? Or perhaps you know you can and need to do something but don't know what to do or how to do it?

When we speak about peace, we mean both interpersonal peace (between individuals) but also personal (internal) serenity or calm. *You can only fully be at peace with yourself when you have expressed your views in some fashion.* The word peace itself derives from a word meaning "agreement, reconciliation, covenant, or permission."[15]

Grace and her boss weren't seeing eye to eye because they had phone and email discussions that went something like this: her boss would ask her to do something, and she would consent without any pushback.

Most of the time we can't see eye to eye if we don't talk face to face. Even if we can't speak face to face, you reveal your true "face" when you speak up. Anything less is a mask, or *a false reflection of our feelings.*

The more significant the issue is, the greater the potential benefit from dealing with it. The following expressions also come to mind: I'm glad I got that off my chest, and, it feels like a million pounds was lifted off of me. *The emotional weight of unresolved issues reduces our effectiveness in life.* Creativity, energy, productivity, enjoyment, and personal health are all affected by frustrations left unattended.

The very minute Grace decided to confront her boss, she felt powerful. She felt like herself again. And when she finally did tell her boss how she felt, the fear of what he would say was gone. Why give away the power of expression that is freely yours to use? *You do not require any additional validation to show that you have feelings and thoughts like any other human being.*

Why Should We Confront?

Reason #7 - Personal Growth

Let me be clear here, we are now pointing the finger inward, at ourselves, and not outward. We need to look in the mirror and tell ourselves what must change. We must also learn to accept feedback from others. Other people may not be out to get you in the way that you are imagining. It may be that some of what others are saying to you scares you because it resonates within you. It may be that we are afraid to admit that we need to make some changes. After all, change can be scary. But the reality is that stagnation is just as frightening. Unresolved issues lead to negative behaviors that impede a fulfilling life.

Most likely the negative patterns in your life have their roots inside of you, and not just those around you. Allowing your perspectives and behavior to be confronted, by yourself, and under the right circumstances can be liberating. Dealing with our problems happens when we look at our actions and acknowledge the need for change. Every person holds beliefs that must be addressed to bring about change and personal growth. These ideas create an internal conflict between what you want to do and what you do. You find that you want to behave in one way, and yet you do the opposite. Pattern behaviors (as we will touch upon) are initiated by both beliefs and our past experiences that create them.

Past conflicts, painful or confusing experiences, and traumatic events by nature demand some reckoning. By that, we mean that people naturally seek to identify why something has happened. More specifically, *why did this happen to me?* The danger with internalizing these conflicts (as opposed to talking about them with others, or dealing with them head-on) is that we are far more likely to draw the wrong conclusions about why something happened. We may take that belief and begin to make decisions about ourselves and our future based on it. *Perhaps most interesting is that the very nature of confrontation and conflict-averse behavior is that not only does it not reduce stress or make issues go away, but instead it creates and enforces damaging patterns of behavior.*

Take Jane for instance. Abandoned by her mother at birth, she becomes a ward of the state. Eventually, a loving family adopts her. She struggles to be a part of any group permanently. Deep inside she has questions about her validity. Jane secretly holds the belief that she was "no good." Or take perhaps Kate, abandoned by her father at 6, and her mother dies a short time after. She lives afraid of losing another person she loves and subconsciously derails every relationship in her life that progresses beyond being an acquaintance. The traumatic event (good or bad) creates beliefs that become a part of both the individual's self-image and worldview. Your view of the world is a sum of your deeply held beliefs. The same danger exists even when we are older or with less severe events. A simple pattern of rejection several times over - by peers, family, or co-workers can affect a person's views and cause them to question themselves. The result of this questioning might be unwanted emotions, personal instability, and a downward spiral of bad behaviors.

Avoiding conflict does not reduce the stress from issues, but instead empowers it to create damaging patterns of behavior.

The very nature of confrontation and conflict-averse behavior is that not only does it not reduce stress or make issues go away, but instead it creates and enforces damaging patterns. These lead to more stress, can reinforce low self-esteem, and translate into social and economic immobility or decline. The result of these behaviors is degraded thinking, which manifests itself as reduced intelligence, lack of creativity, an inability to think logically, and a lack of initiative and motivation. While many "confrontational" individuals may exhibit these negative characteristics, the reality is that they are most likely *not engaging in a healthy form of confrontation*, but rather *lashing out*. Lashing out is a reaction to some prior trauma or interpersonal conflict.

Out of bounds, reactionary behavior reveals the pre-existence of internal conflicts. The focus of this book is interpersonal and intrapersonal harmony. Our goal for every confrontation is to create peace.

Even the very decision to confront someone can bring immediate relief. Your brain finds rest when it sees an end to a troubling situation ahead. *The moment you decide to do something, your mind can marshal its resources to help you achieve it.* Merely choosing to deal with it releases a good feeling (hope) and stops the negative emotions associated with the issue.

When we confront others, we seek to come to an agreement or a mutual understanding. Shared understanding doesn't imply that we agree on everything, but that we understand where we agree, where we differ, and how we can accept the differences. One benefit of learning to confront is getting to this place of shared understanding.

We have seen some examples of how leaving things unresolved creates worse situations. We have also evaluated the positive outcomes that come from resolving them. Learning to deal with our problems (and those of others) has many benefits. Issues can be resolved if we try. We gain a sense of control over our lives and fulfillment. We increase our self-esteem. We create peace within ourselves and with others. We live a better life emotionally, mentally, and physically. We help others to grow and learn, and develop ourselves in the process. We overcome rejection, anger, stress, and frustration. We make society a better place to live and preserve valuable relationships. We are more likely to be successful financially. These are some of the many reasons that we need to learn to deal with it and confront.

Confrontation contributes to a healthy life, healthy relationships and healthy perspectives. We also have seen why those who seek to embrace and master the art of "dealing with it" have a more fulfilling life. *Confrontation is a necessary and helpful part of communication, and it is also a part of self-examination.* When head-on analysis and the engagement of chaos (daily issues) becomes a pattern, it can reach all of society with its effects. The challenge of how to begin this kind of life, and how to engage our issues is what we will turn our focus to in the following chapters.

3

ROLES, REACTIONS, AND RESPONSES TO CONFLICT

In this chapter, we will deal with how people behave. We will look at the roles they live in, how and why they may react to others (and us), in a certain way, and look at how we can respond to these roles and reactions.

CAST OF CHARACTERS

Have you ever felt unjustly labeled? Perhaps somebody said something about you in elementary or middle school, and it just stuck with you (and maybe with them) for too long? Numerous studies have been conducted demonstrating that how we perceive and label others determine what we expect of them, and broadly how we treat them. Some of these studies reveal that just by labeling people, we cast them in a role that is hard for them to break.[1] Since this is a book about overcoming our limitations, we need to begin to remove limiting labels and take a posture of fluidity or mutability. That is, to believe that as individuals we can all improve, learn, and change. What a person does, or has done, is not the final definition of that person. We use the term roles to indicate that the same way an actor is not the character or part they play, people can be separated from their actions. Separating a person from their actions can be essential for us to deal with that person appropriately. When we value the individual apart from their behavior, we can react (and assess our reactions) to that person out of love and not based on their actions alone. We can value the potential and future of that person just as we also must value our future and potential.

Our goals here are to illustrate behavior (and not permanently cast characters), to examine how and why a person can act out a commonly observed drama. We are defining their behavior, and not the individual. We are all prone to act out, and truthfully we are all in some stage of personal growth. The reason we try to understand these behaviors is to not only deal with them when confronted by them, but to avoid them in our lives and rout the causes of them in our lives as well.

Remember: You are not your behavior, but you are the person managing your response. We must learn to control our reactions if we want to improve our lives and the quality of our conversations. One of the first steps to managing our behavior is to become self-aware. If you see any of these behaviors in yourself, you will be at the first step of change.

Not just sentiments, but symptoms

The questions we should ask are: "What makes a person behave the way they do?" and "Why do we do what we do?" Every behavior has a reason, a cause. Every problem behavior has origins. The Law of Cause and Effect can be witnessed in all of life. Through numerous studies, psychologists have shown how the formative years of an individual create relational dynamics and a sense of identity that is often in place for life.[2] Only by adjusting the sense of self and dealing with the causes of emotional triggers can we change the reactions common to ourselves.

The Past and Patterns: Wounds, Scars, and Memories

While some patterns from the past can have tremendous benefits once understood and applied, others are detrimental pattern behaviors that obfuscate the truth, hinder personal growth, stifle careers, and ruin relationships. These thought systems, false ideas, and outright lies must be recognized for the troublemakers that they are. Until the victim of these lies comes to awareness, they will not be able to make a dramatic change.

Watch out for the Bombs! Avoid or Diffuse?

There are some behaviors that we can avoid triggering in others, and others that we can diffuse once triggered. It can be challenging to deal with certain people, but as much as it is possible, we want to live in peace with our neighbors. True peace is not a two-faced avoidance of conflict but settling issues and finding common ground in mutual understanding. There are some people perhaps that it is beyond our scope to help and that is also OK.

Peace is not a two-faced avoidance of conflict but settling issues and finding common ground and mutual understanding.

I once read a story of how Confucius was traveling on the road with his disciples. As they went on, they encountered a man who was going to the bathroom just off of the way. Confucius stopped and rebuked the man for being in plain sight. Just a short while later in their travels, they came upon another man who was going to the bathroom in the middle of the road. Confucius led his disciples straight on past the man without even stopping. His followers were puzzled by this and asked him why he did not say anything to the second man when he had rebuked the first. Confucius exclaimed, "That second fellow is crazy, there is no sense in trying to reason with him. The first fellow at least had enough sense to be on the side of the road." While not everyone can be "reasoned with," it is far too often we fail to address those that will hear what we have to say.

Pattern Interruption

The term 'pattern interrupt' is often used to define a method of stopping the initiated or cyclical behavior in conversations, relationships, and daily living. This concept has been used by countless life coaches and counselors for decades and attributed mainly to psychologist Milton Erikson.[3] The goal of these techniques is to break the ingrained and seemingly unconscious harmful habits that people seem to do without thought. Stopping mindless eating would be one example. A more relevant case would be the reactions that people have to certain things. A boss who yells every time someone comes into his office, a co-worker who goes ballistic every time they are asked for a status on something, perhaps ranting about all of the catastrophes that have happened in the last 24 hours. Interrupting these patterns is necessary for gaining any short-term changes in outcome when dealing with established behaviors.

Erickson's theory is based on the premise that by interrupting an ingrained social behavior, he could gain access to a person's subconscious or at least some metacognitive state of hyper-awareness. Erickson viewed this state as quasi-hypnotic or possibly a weak trance. By breaking a chain of events in a series of subconsciously programmed actions (such as the handshake) he could quickly gain the full attention of his patients while also derailing their programmed responses and social inhibitions. Silencing these inhibitions allowed the client to address the real issues in therapy and let the therapist help them to re-program their behavior. The Pattern Interrupt technique is often a part of Neuro-Linguistic Programming or NLP.[4]

The way we can apply this to confrontation is by doing something different than what is expected, perhaps the opposite. Naming the behavior is one of these techniques. Let's say that Jim is trying to get a reaction out of Billy. Billy, being aware of this tactic, can call it out by saying, "It seems like you are trying to provoke me." Jim will be forced to think about it. Where possible we will insert some strategies or examples here as well as in the later chapters. Often these are simple statements like, "Wow, it sounds like this is important to you," or "I'm sorry, could you repeat that?"

Creating new patterns

More important for long-term growth and progression in life is the decision-action-discipline principle* for creating new behaviors. This principle can be defined as a process where a person recognizes the need for change and willingly decides to make that change, takes immediate action, and reviews and monitors activity and behavior with a conscious effort to stick to the decision.[5]

Creating new behavior patterns has been the thrust of counseling, coaching, success, and self-help for longer than we can record - well over 100 years and beyond.

The pitfalls of trying to change micro behavior by micro behavior are many. Creating a new self-image (a view and perspective of self) or a new identity is ultimately the best way to short-circuit these pitfalls. When we are sure of who we are, we will prefer or take actions consistent with that identity or self-image by default.

How does one begin to create a new identity? While we haven't set out to deal with that topic in this book, I will lay out a few commonly accepted points. Spend time dreaming, imagining, and thinking about the ideal you. Meditating on this "ideal you" allows you to become that person. The qualities and nature of this "future you" will begin to dictate your habits, actions, and behaviors. Evaluate your expressions and motives and see how they line up with that new you. Catch yourself and tune yourself by learning to become self-aware. We should not become overwhelmed if we see some of the following dysfunctional behaviors in our life, but strengthen our resolve to build a new picture of who we are and find new ways to respond to our environment.

"We are what we repeatedly do. Excellence then is not an act, but a habit." -Aristotle

What Color are Your Hot Spots? - And what to do when you feel your temperature rise. *Signature Stress Response*

When a stressful situation arises, when you are stretched emotionally, or physically, what do you do? If someone gets in our business, how do we respond? Are you more susceptible to flight or fight behaviors of a particular type? It is no secret that many people have signature responses to specific stressors. When stressors trigger these signature responses, the individual is acting out some established patterns of behavior that are specifically stress induced.[6] Today's fast-paced society and stressful lifestyles have spawned new levels of stress and corresponding relational dysfunction. When stress levels are consistently toxic, then poor communication and these behaviors often become an ingrained pattern or lifestyle. Since stress management is often a lifestyle issue, lifestyle changes can be a powerful contributing factor when they accompany any effort to improve our communication. Simple strategies will not be enough for permanent progress (in the case of constant stress build up), but will undoubtedly help while dealing with both lifestyle and underlying causation. Examining some of the more commonly known Signature Stress Responses will help to better understand your current personal communication strategies and those of others, as well as ingrained safety mechanisms such as communication avoidance.

Personal communication behaviors and safety mechanisms often manifest in conversations as Defensive or Thwarting tactics brought on by existing insecurity, painful examinations, past failures, or momentary physical strain such as tiredness, exhaustion, or sickness. Even hunger and poor diet can make us "hangry," or cranky.

While text, internet, and social media have made tremendous advancements in our modes, methods, and reach of communication, they have also impacted the way, styles, and skills with which we communicate. The more problematic communication behaviors from these media can creep into our other modes and channels that are more intimate and sabotage our ability, and our confidence, when face to face with others. Perhaps this is why we have heard reports of Millennials asking bosses to "text me my employee review." Laughable as it sounds, it is a symptom of aversion to confrontation. It says, "I don't want to deal with this."

Remember Jim, the husband who acted to defend himself by verbally assaulting his wife every time she came with a list of requests or what he perceived were complaints? He had fallen into a trap - a pattern of aggressive defensiveness. Saving his marriage, improving his live, and being happy all depend on his ability to break this pattern, and respond differently. Without a doubt the web of angst is likely affecting other areas of his life as well.

Defensive and Thwarting tactics

Most of our learned strategies for avoiding difficult conversations developed in childhood and have been used ever since.[7] These behaviors are intended to protect the individual from what feels to be an attack. The truth is, however, that most often the individual is not under attack and their defense mechanisms are doing little to help them.

For example, you need to speak to someone about being late, or some minor grievance and these are the responses:

One person begins to cry
Another has a sob story of tragedies
They change the subject of the conversation to faults of the accuser
Justification of behavior by some means.

Any behavior other than taking responsibility and apologizing is ultimately a defensive tactic to avoid the pain of failure.

Let's look at traditional roles.

CAST OF CHARACTERS

1. Self Pity/Poor Me Syndrome (PMS)
Victimized Victor. Disadvantaged Daisy.

PMS is where an emotional plea of helplessness, inability, or claims of being at a factual disadvantage are all the response to confrontation. These characteristics become the defense mechanism of those who cling to victimization as their means of justification, or seek pity from others for their situation to deny or deflect responsibility for their behavior. They may classically try to make it appear that they have no real choice with regards to their behavior, or are powerless because of their circumstances. Most often they seek to justify why they should not have to concede or change their position, course of action or opinion based on some set of tragic or less than optimal circumstances in which they have found themselves. They are possibly the victim of life, society, or merely several continual mishaps. They are looking for their break in life instead of working to break their cycle. The problem with this unrealistic hope is that losers seldom catch a break.

In some case, you may have to go parental on these childish statements and put the goals and outcomes out in front. Get them to affirm that they want the results of different behavior and that personal change (responsibility, maturity) is necessary to achieve those outcomes. In other words, quit whining and do what you know you must.

One example of this behavior and dealing with it comes from the classic TV show, *The Waltons*. Elizabeth Walton graduates from high school and becomes distressed because she doesn't know what she wants to pursue. She compares herself to everyone in her class and her siblings, who all seem to have some outstanding talent or abilities, while she feels that she has none. Elizabeth becomes withdrawn and complains to her older brother how she can't do anything right. Her brother points out that the only person she can seem to think about is herself and that is her first problem. Receiving this rebuke, Elizabeth decides to do something for her brother and secretly takes a second job at a business school to buy him the typewriter he needs for his work. In so doing she accidentally finds out that she has an aptitude for the job and enrolls in the school as well.[8]

Not only does Elizabeth shift her focus off of herself, and stop pitying herself, and remove excuses, she takes action that makes her feel better. She discovers by trying to do something for her brother that she has skills she can put to use. Seeing this not only makes her happier, but it also causes her to grow as a person, improve her self-esteem, and her communication. By confronting her, her brother helped to break this pattern of self pity. This story illustrates that it is possible to reason with those who will listen and that the defense mechanism Elizabeth had was hurting her, instead of helping her.

When confronting PMS, it is vital to get agreement around these three things;

1. What is it that Victimized Victor and Disadvantaged Daisy want? Is what they are seeking reasonable and are they going about getting it in the right way? Can they describe their behavior, and what would be a better response or course of action? You can do this by having them look at the situation in someone else's shoes. Try using a parable or a similar story.

2. Illustrate that the outcome that DD and VV want will come by doing what is right, or something that they are refusing to do; i.e. taking appropriate action, accepting responsibility.

3. Help those with PMS to understand the choices they have. Once they acknowledge that, then they can also do the right thing to achieve reasonable outcomes.

Once you have established this line of reasoning, get them to agree to the appropriate action and be committed to acting on it immediately. The key in the example of Elizabeth was her immediate action to change her outlook and prevent procrastination. Use coaching and encouragement of the most basic form to nudge people along. "I know you can do it," and "You are going to feel so much better once you do this."

Cognitive behavioral therapist, Haley Elder, M.A., describes PMS as self-piteous cognitions and verbal declarations a.k.a. the "poor me" phenomenon, where one globally labels others as well as life/the world at large as harsh, cruel, and unfair for treating them unjustly.[9]

We can see by the above that those suffering from this emotional disease see themselves as powerless victims.

Elder goes on to conclude that: 'By stewing in hatred of others and life, one is perpetuating their misery... One's chronic insistence that life circumstances (should) change and (that) others (should) behave differently towards them as well as the whiny rehearsal of self-talk like "others and life are bad because they don't give me what I want" does nothing but self-defeat and propagate negative, unhealthy states of being. Chronic depression and unremitting rage flourish within this frame of mind.[10]

The heart knows its bitterness, and a stranger does not share its joy.

Book of Proverbs 14:10

Each person has their struggle and challenges to face. Often life can be difficult and people even worse. Nevertheless, there are good people, good days, and things worth living for. Focusing on what you can't change will always leave you feeling hopeless. Concentrating on what you can control will allow you to find opportunities for growth, advancement, and achievement in life. We all must work to identify and act on those opportunities to improve our lives and the lives of others.

To demand that things outside of your control should be different is a poor investment of time and focus.

2. Guilt (Trip) Inducer - GI Jane and GI Joe

Guilt Trip as defined by Oxford Dictionary;

Make (someone) feel guilty, especially to induce them to do something: a pay increase will not guilt-trip them into improvements.

Guy Winch, Ph.D., of Psychology Today defines a guilt trip as a form of verbal or nonverbal communication in which a guilt inducer tries to induce guilty feelings in a target, to control their behavior. He concludes that "guilt trips are a clear form of psychological manipulation and coercion."[11]

Even though a guilt trip may allow the GI to get what they want, it almost certainly will leave others resenting the GI and their tactics.

A guilt trip only works if the person who is on the receiving end allows it to work. By recognizing it for what it is, you can easily see both the intent and why you should not comply with the G.I.'s request or desired outcome. Those who are weak in their ability to discipline, say no, or challenge the selfish nature of the party will find themselves swayed, conned and duped. This could be a weak boss or teacher/ leader known as a softie, a person who is considered to be a pushover.

Research has shown that the Guilt Inducer (the one using the tactic) is usually totally oblivious to its harmful effects (on their relationships) because they are self-focused and therefore uncaring and unaware of others altogether.

G.I.'s may often try this tactic with those they are most familiar with and often repeatedly use a past failure or position actions as infractions to have extortion rights. They use these extortion rights as part of their argument. Holding a person's mistakes over their head is just one example of how G.I.'s try to get what they want.

Alternatively, they may position things they have done as great favors and go the extra mile for you so that you are indebted. They use these as bargaining chips.

They may also compare you to others that they see as a standard and justification for what they want. "Look at so and so, they never, or they seem to," etc.

And last in their bag of tricks is their atom bomb, *the ultimatum*. They may throw some crazy statement - "see if I ever do x,y,z for you again." Or threats of future doom - "when you are down and out you will remember this" - as their closing argument. These individuals will go to any length to get their way and are furious when others refuse to comply with their demands.

Dealing with G.I. Jane

First, honestly explain why you can't and what's at stake. Put them in your shoes. Call them out on the benefits they are seeking and why they are not worth the level of effort, risk and relational capital at stake. Illustrate how they are making you feel. Even more, you may be able to show them that it's not necessarily what they have asked for that bothers you most, but rather that they seek to manipulate you into doing it. If all else fails, then just give them a flat out no - end of discussion and walk away. This derails the pattern. They hope to go to great lengths to get you to comply and will attempt to hold you hostage until you do. This is a poisonous behavior and moreover, if you agree with some ridiculous demands, you will be opening the door for all kinds of resentment from others - either family members at home or team members and employees if at work.

Long term, this individual will need to realize that their behavior is ruining their relationships. Again, the fact may be that what they want might not always be a big deal, but how they ask often is. Furthermore, they need to learn to accept that not everything has to go their way for them to be happy in life. Explain that if they want respect, they need to respect boundaries, that people have a right to make their own decisions, and that includes saying, "no."

You could further explain that their tactics create patterns of avoidance, withdrawal, resentment, and could lead to rejection, abandonment, or retaliation from others. It is not sustainable. Show them that by always looking to profit at the expense of others they can never hope to grow or increase in the long term.

Above all else, we need to coach and live by the golden rule of success. If you focus on doing what is right and best for others, you will find your career advanced and your life satisfying. If you will just do to others as you would like them to do to you, treat others how you want to be treated, and with genuine good towards them for their success, you will find that success continually comes your way.

When they try to throw their crazy tactics, call them out on it. If they threaten it - call it out as a threat. If they give you an ultimatum, restate that you will not be coerced. If they bring up some mistake from the past, let them know that it's old news, you are over it, and so is everyone else.

A fear of not having control over every situation needs to be addressed. Life is not about controlling others but ourselves. The real test is to maintain your composure and choose how you will represent yourself even when things don't go your way. Control is exhibited by being at peace with the fact that other opinions exist, and being able to accept that people typically don't do what you want. One sign of a strong internal locus of control is the ability to control your behavior.

3. Flying Off the Handle - Bobby OR (Over-Reactor)

To fly off the handle essentially means to lose control of one's self.

This American phrase alludes to the uncontrolled way a loose ax-head flies off from its handle.

"He flies right off the handle for nothing."

"Fly off the handle" is a term used to describe what happens when someone reacts in a way that is wild and unchecked.

It could be sudden uncontrolled anger or loud outbursts. This is also known as overreacting. When the emotional intensity and severity of someone's behavior doesn't match the situation at hand, they are overreacting.

Relationship expert, Dr. Julie Hanks, describes two kinds of OR behavior: Internal and External. She defines external overreactions as emotional tirades, outbursts, and sometimes wild behavior that may include slamming or breaking objects, yelling, and insults. Conversely, internal overreactions would be emotional responses that remain inside of a person without others necessarily being aware of the impact.[13] Examples of internal overreactions are mental fixation; i.e. thinking about the situation, replaying the events in one's mind, and feeling those same emotions with intensity - all internally. Often these are negative, toxic and strong emotions. Feeding this kind of pattern can pose significant health risks and cause stress to wreak havoc on the body, creating negativity and further dysfunction in daily life. Additionally, it is more than likely that at some point these internal reactions lead to extreme actions - either an outburst, fleeing, passive-aggressive vengeance or some other dramatic behavior.

Dealing with OR

If you are confronted by someone's external emotional tirade: Warning: Do Not Enter! It's a trap!

The person who overreacts usually views the present situation as leading to the catastrophic outcome. Their belief about the severity of conditions may cause them to react severely. Additionally, this could be a pattern behavior. Whenever they feel that their safety or sense of control is threatened, they may use this tactic as their emotional go-to. Since this kind of extreme behavior can be dangerous, it is best if you don't engage unless you have to.

If you do have to engage, you can try to postpone addressing the situation, assuming they can respond rationally in some way.

What to Say: Call a time-out. Yes, make the 'T' Symbol. Ask the Ticking Time Bomb to stop. Request that he or she refrain from the wild behavior by naming it explicitly. There is no need to: yell, shout, sweat, etc.

Rather than springing a conversation on him or her, request a time that you could sit down and chat. I want to hear you out, let me just take care of this (insert some situation), and then we can talk. I will call/text/email you in a little bit to figure out what works. When later comes, you will need to explain how you felt that the outburst was unwarranted and how it made you uncomfortable. It may be good to make sure that they are rational and perhaps meet them in a public place or speak by phone. If in any way you are concerned about your safety, never meet with someone in distress alone.

What to say when you do meet? Something simple like, "I understand that sometimes we all lose our cool" is a good lead-in.

If you must deal with the individual presently, try to understand what it is that they want, and if it's possible, point to a way that they can get resolution. For instance, they may say, "If such and such doesn't happen, then I will…" If you can point to a resolution, they may act on it and be out of your hands.

A word on Anger

Leonard Ingram, of the Anger Institute of Chicago, reports that one out of five Americans has an anger management problem.[14] Failure to manage anger is one of the major causes of conflict in our personal and professional relationships.

Dealing with Anger

Anger is a natural human emotional response, and it can be justified. Feeling angry (or upset) in and of itself is not necessarily the problem. It is what we do with the feeling that is the real issue at hand. Unchecked anger will lead to unhealthy attitudes and actions. The problem is not so much that you feel agitated, but that in pride you have become judge, jury, and executioner of the person you are angry with. Once you have condemned this person in your heart and mind, the chances are that you will now act on it. Some examples could be to belittle, berate, and slander this person. In reality, it is quite likely that the feelings directed at someone may have very little to do with the present situation or that person in front of us. Other frustrations or personal triggers may be driving our reactions. Try asking yourself these questions:

What is the reason I am upset?
Is there something else that is bothering me?
How should I respond here - and if the situation was reversed, what would I want the other person to do?

These same questions can be altered to use with someone overreacting or upset. For example:

"It seems like you are upset. Can we talk about it?"

The next time you get upset, take time to examine the real cause of your feelings, as well as to put yourself in the other person's shoes. Don't act immediately if you are upset, and don't move without thinking about the consequences of your actions in advance. Above all, try to calm down. Anger clouds our ability to think clearly, and makes it difficult for us to see the obvious. When we are upset with what someone has said or done, many times, we are likely wrong about their motives. We may respond with a severity that is uncalled for.

Often, if left undealt with, anger builds. Wrath is a term used for extreme anger put into action. This word comes from the idea of something that is twisting us up inside as it builds. In other cases, anger festers when it is not dealt with. This kind of anger can grow, lying latent until triggered, until it bursts out uncontrollably. Irritation can lead to angry perspectives and:

Blame shifting
Accusations and throwing stones
Being overly defensive

The Pressure Pan. Often related to over-reacting is the Pressure Pan Syndrome. This behavior is seen when a person holds every emotion inside until the last possible moment and then explodes. Like a pressure pan that either must blow up or let off steam, this person may or may not show signs of impending danger. We must learn to deal with situations by talking about them as they come, rather than allowing emotions to become pent up in ourselves or others when we know that they are upset with us. We should go to them and address the issue because it is the right thing to do.

Most people who choose not to express themselves do so out of any number of false hopes and beliefs. They may be afraid of the outcome or how others will view them. Often, insecurities drive people to seek the approval of others. This constant need to be "liked" by others puts them in fear of the reactions of these same people. Because of weak self-esteem, they are afraid to risk any potential damage to their self-image. Most often they experience this damage when others are upset with them. They may feel that they are worthless, or a failure. When it comes to conflicts, they hope that the other party gives up, that things work out for them. They will imagine any possible outcome or use nearly any justification to keep them from having to confront others. They are afraid of confrontation and will avoid it at all costs. It usually costs them every opportunity to do good to others because they value their comfort above the truth. This type of avoidance may also present itself as being aloof, self-absorbed and unaware of reality. Some justifications may include: "I don't think he/she/they will listen," or "it won't do any good." Both are excuses and usually wrong.

Those with a low EQ have difficulty perceiving reactions well and rely on their perspective to find solutions instead of asking others. The truth: most of the time there is no reason we should have to assume the feelings of others, especially of people we know well. We should be able to find some way to ask them directly and know for sure. There is no point in worrying that they won't tell us. If they do tell us, we gain understanding, deepen the relationship, and establish trust. If they don't tell us, then we illustrate our good intent and begin to build the bridge, but are likely no worse off. If they lie to us, then we will discover that they may have fears and issues that are causing them to be untrustworthy. Remember, it is not always what you ask a person that affects their response, but how you ask that matters most.

What to do when you are really mad, angry or upset?

Do not act on it! The emotional brain does not make good decisions!
Walk away.
Take a time out.
Go for a run or to the gym and get some exercise.
Talk about it with yourself by journaling or recording a memo on your phone and then listen to how you sound. Erase it and repeat until you are calm.

Try to put yourself in the other person's shoes - have compassion and don't assume anything about the situation. Take deep breaths and count backwards.

Squeeze yourself by wrapping your arms across your chest and hugging yourself for 10 seconds. Repeat until you feel tired.

Talk to a counselor you trust.

Analyze why you are so upset and put it in a larger context to reduce its impact and size.

4. PA System: The Passive Aggressor

What is Passive Aggression?

Daniel K. Hall-Flavin, M.D., states that "Passive-aggressive behavior is a pattern of indirectly expressing negative feelings instead of openly addressing them." Dr. Hall-Flavin further says that passive-aggressive people express their negative feelings harmfully, but indirectly.[15]

When what a person says is not reflected by what he or she does, that is passive-aggression. While potentially saying, "everything is great," they may be upset or frustrated and acting out of that emotion in secret.

Passive-aggressive people hide their aggression to appear passive.

Identifying Passive-Aggressive Behavior

Some signs of passive-aggressive behavior from an individual:

He or she shuts down or shuts themselves out

Agrees to do something but never does it (procrastination and making excuses)

Distractive behavior

Shifting responsibility to others when it is rightfully theirs

Complains about feeling under-appreciated or cheated

"Memory lapses"

Irritability, and a cynical or hostile attitude: hostile jokes, sarcastic remarks

The silent treatment: "I won't get angry. I'll get even."

The silent treatment is a symptom of bad communication skills and immaturity. It usually doesn't solve anything.

PA's attempt to hide how they are feeling to avoid conflict. Perhaps poor communication skills have ruined confrontation for them in the past, or they may lack self-confidence. Either way, they have not learned how to directly and calmly express themselves tactfully.

If you're not encouraged to be open and honest about your feelings from an early age, you might use passive-aggressive behavior as an alternative to addressing issues head-on. For example, you might sulk, withdraw from people emotionally, or find indirect ways to communicate how you feel.

People may act like this because they fear losing control, or lack self-esteem. They might do it to cope with stress, anxiety, depression, or insecurity, or to deal with rejection or conflict. Alternatively, they might do it because they have a grudge against a colleague, or feel under-appreciated.

Passive-aggression can be the reaction of choice—especially when bullied—because we don't want to incur further wrath from the bully by overtly and directly challenging the beast.[16]

PA's are afraid of confrontation because they either have been traumatized by that kind of action in the past, or they fear that they will not remain composed themselves.

Dealing with PA's

Identify the Cause

Identifying the cause of the behavior may take some patience as PA's will need coaxing before telling you how they feel. You may need to call it out by stating, "It seems like you are not performing at your best lately. Did I do something to upset you?" Or "It seems like something is off, and I want to ask if it is a result of something I have done?" It may take several phases of gentle question asking to get to the bottom. Remember, these individuals are most likely to resist speaking up in the first place.

Setting Boundaries

Confront passive-aggressive behavior in person to make sure your communication is understood, as opposed to using indirect means like email.

Passive aggressiveness isn't always easy to spot. In order to prevent this kind of behavior, you must constantly work to foster regular direct dialog where people feel safe and can be honest.

If you notice PA, then you should address it directly. Stay calm during your conversation, and ask questions to find out the reasons behind your team member's actions so you can deal with them.

Key Phrases, Statements and Questions

I've noticed that you are awfully silent lately. Is something bothering you?

Is there any particular reason that you haven't been participating in the conversation? We would love to hear your opinion (ideas, input), and get your feedback even if you're not sure it will make sense. We need to hear from you so that we get your perspective.

You are a part of this team/family. Don't be afraid to speak up. We can handle it (*yes, you can handle it*).

What if you are the one who is acting passive aggressive?

You must speak up. Write out your thoughts if needed. Let others know that you want to share but are afraid that it will be misunderstood, or not go well. *Being vulnerable is being brave.* Be brave. When you start with honesty, people are more likely to listen attentively. Remember, it is not good to hold it in, to keep grudges, or to think of others as the enemy. Ask yourself, "why am I afraid?" Read the guide in Chapter 5! Start small. You can begin to build your confidence by speaking up in casual conversations. By taking small steps, you can grow in this area.

Working to get everyone on the same page and hold each other accountable for being forthright is a job that will require persistent action.

The Assassin (Back Stabbers, Slanderers, Character Assassins)

Also known as a back channeler, these types usually organize a "set up." These characters pre-arrange a coup by spreading their story to gain the support of others before confronting you. Using back channels (private or slanderous conversations), they hide and cover up their trail. Their hope is to expose you and vindicate themselves at the same time. They may or may not realize that their methods are immoral, and may not care. Their dark and slippery way creates a path of destruction. A word to the wise comes from the following ancient proverbs:

The first to state his case seems right until his opponent begins to cross-examine him. (Proverbs 18:17).

The one who answers before he listens-- this is foolishness and disgrace for him. (Proverbs 18:13).

Let all of the facts come out before passing judgment. This type of character is related to passive aggression in that it uses deception to covertly operate and draw others into the scheme. It should be dealt with immediately by asking appropriate questions. You can often identify when someone has slandered you because people who have heard the untruthful report change or cut off their communication with you, often without explanation. You must try to find out who has slandered you and address them directly. Using the guide in Chapter 5 will help you know what to say.

Another variant of this technique is commonly known as character assassination. This tactic is where a person attempts to discredit another with personal attacks to their face. Character assassination includes direct verbal attacks such as name calling, disparaging comments, or again, pointing out of faults.

How to handle it? Name calling is explicitly a form of bullying, which we address more below. However, it can be dealt with directly either now, or later depending on whether the person doing the name calling is acting rationally. Being direct and honest without losing your cool is the best way to respond.

Please stop calling names. There is no reason to call people names.

I find it insulting or hurtful when people resort to name calling. Let's focus on the situation at hand.

Can you describe the things that you are upset about without using name calling?

5. Bullies: Dealing with Bullies

To bully someone is to treat them abusively. Bullying happens when a bully tries to get you to do what they want (against your will or inclination) using force or coercion. Often this is through the use of browbeating language or behavior best described as blustering.

According to the United States Government, those who bully use their power—such as physical strength, access to embarrassing information, or popularity—to control or harm others. Power imbalances can change over time and in different situations, even if they involve the same people.[17]

Bullying is repeated, aggressive behavior that can be physical, verbal, or relational. Bullies use intimidation to make those they bully afraid and to dominate them for their purposes.

Bullies may often do their best to make sure that those they bully feel to blame for their aggressive behavior, that it's somehow their fault. Those who have been bullied feel hurt, angry, afraid, helpless, hopeless, isolated, ashamed, and guilty.

Bullying behavior can include:

Isolating behavior: Refusing to talk to someone, exclusion from groups or activities.
Defamation: Spreading lies or rumors about someone.
Hazing: Includes pushing, shoving, throwing things, and other mild to severe physical aggression.

Harassment: Continual and repeated acts of intimidation.
Public and private humiliation: Name calling, derogatory and debasing statements, revealing sensitive personal information.
Coercion: Making someone do things he or she doesn't want to do.

I have met some genuine bullies, but I have also seen someone who is not a bully lose it and harass another person inappropriately. Neither is okay. I bring this up to say that everyone deserves a chance. If it is your first experience with someone and they seem to be a bully, it may be okay to walk away, shake it off, and see what happens next. They may cool down, change their behavior or even apologize. Even if they do apologize, it still requires something from you to let them know that they:

Are forgiven but have crossed the line.
May need help dealing with issues, emotions or life.

If a person repeats this behavior, you must stand up to them. If they are threatening you, then you should try to document how, when, and where the events took place and report it to someone who can help you. If they have threatened your personal space and are overly aggressive, you may need to report it to the police.

Protect yourself. There is nothing wrong with defending yourself from a physical assault. Your course of action should be first to try to escape. Next, you should report it to police or other authority figures. If there is no escape, then defending yourself is a must. Your goal is to protect yourself and escape, not to exact justice on the bully.

You may be familiar with the classic show, *Little House on the Prairie*. There is one particular episode that gives us a picture of bullying.[18]

The three Galender brothers come into town. Consisting of two men and a teenage boy, they take advantage of everyone through various bullying tactics. They buy things at the local mill and town store on credit and then don't pay. They undercut a deal that was already agreed to by some of the townspeople, and the youngest pushes around the other kids at school, including punching the girls. The townspeople air their grievances to Reverend Alden. Reverend Alden meets with the brothers, who claim to be honest men, who tell a story (which later turns out to be a lie) about how they have suffered family difficulty and need a break. In light of this, the Reverend asks the townspeople to give them a chance, but it soon becomes clear the Galenders are lying.

It goes from bad to worse when the men harass a woman while walking to town. When her husband, Charles, confronts them, the brothers gang up on him and beat him up. Reverend Alden's eyes open, and he invites the brothers to church, where the people "rise up" and chase them out of town.

Bullies thrive off of control and the fear of others. This power cycle is usually learned from another abuser or bully who has subjected the bully to intimidation and held them under their control using intimidation tactics. A bully knows that they can only maintain their power when they have a unique advantage. Their singular position typically can only remain secure by trying to keep those they intimidate from broadcasting the truth about their bullying. They usually threaten worse abuse if they are exposed. A bully needs to keep their behavior hidden to maintain power. That is why exposing a bully is the key to stopping their abuse.

The lesson learned is that sometimes when there's trouble in your midst, you have to deal with it directly and immediately. You must confront it head-on.

Moral Courage is revealed in the ability to say and do the right thing regardless of the implications. An act takes courage if it is uncomfortable or done in spite of fear. Irrespective of conflicting forces and danger, the courageous act out of unwavering convictions and without personal concern. The only real way to stop the bullying is to expose it by telling people about it. This means specifically telling those in a position of authority, like coaches, bosses, teachers, security or law enforcement.

Many movies and television shows have shown both bullies and what happens when they are left unchecked as well as what happens when we confront them. One of these is the film *Back to the Future*.[19]

In the 80's classic, *Back to the Future*, Marty McFly travels back in time and witnesses his parents in their teen years. Since we have already had a glimpse of his parents at the start of the movie, we know how they turned out. Something unexpected happens, however, as Marty interacts with his parents (who are unaware he is their future son) and inadvertently changes the future.

Remember Biff - the bully from *Back to the Future?* He held George McFly under his thumb with his bullying. It wasn't until George finally stood up to Biff that it stopped. Not only did George realize that he could stand up to Biff, but he realized that he could succeed at things he had never done before. The effects for George in this classic tale play out dramatically for him over the long haul. George had two possible futures: one where he remained a submissive dweeb and another where he took risks and reaped the rewards. In the first future he had a bullying manager, a dysfunctional family, and never told anyone his dreams. In the second possible future, George McFly had a healthy family, marriage, fulfilling career, and overcame his fear of failure, following his desire to become a published author. The difference between these two was one decision to pursue the girl of his dreams and in the process confront his bully, Biff. The outcome of these events led to a whole new series of behaviors as well as self-confidence.

Think that you may have bullied others or been perceived as a bully?

You need tactical help. A mentor, manager, or community leader who's held in high regard but has a communication style different from yours. Approach them, seek feedback about your issues and how you are communicating with others. Look to them for cues as to how you can approach conversations and manage your behavior.

There are certainly many other kinds of dysfunctional behaviors and characters. We have taken a look at these simply because they are the most important ones to deal with when overcoming the fear of confrontation. Managing our cast of characters wisely reduces conflicts to discussions.

CHAPTER 4

CONVERSION: DEVELOPING A BETTER LIFE

CONVERSION: DEVELOPING A BETTER LIFE BY BECOMING A BETTER PERSON

"It hurts me when I hear you talk about yourself that way, because I love you, and I see that it's not true. Not only is it not true, but it's holding you back from being who you are."

Maybe you know someone who is always putting themselves down? Psychologists, like Dr. Phil, trace the roots of negative self-talk to personal self-concept, a topic that he thoroughly covers in his book, *Self Matters*. This correlation is also key to the idea behind this chapter. This book can provide you with a formula for success, helpful patterns, and tips for conversations, but in the end, they may fail to work for you for this reason: What you believe about yourself governs your behavior. Your beliefs about yourself can prevent change from happening in your life.

If you believe that you need to be aggressive to get what you want or to avoid being taken advantage of, then you will be aggressive. When we show you how to be gentle or to be patient and listen, you will be challenged to do so, even when we demonstrate the positive outcomes that result from it. While we can't do this topic justice in a single chapter, we can show you how to make progress.

I was just reading an email from a business associate who said, "Things always get lost in my mind." Whether or not this is scientifically possible or plausible doesn't matter. What matters is that he plans to have everything repeated and reiterated while blaming his mind. The real issue is not that his mind is losing things. The real problem is that he fears to make a decision, so he procrastinates. By forcing discussions to ground zero, he avoids the two things that he fears. One is saying yes, and subsequently having to work out the logistics. The second is to say no, even if it's best to say no. The perceived difficulty of having to tell someone "no," is enough. It may be that he fears others will be displeased with him if he tells them, "no." In either case, his inability to deal with decisions frustrates those around him and stalemates his progress in life. Until my friend recognizes his behavior and changes his thinking about decision making, there is not much that can be done to help him avoid the conflicts and confrontations that this pattern will create. He needs a personal transformation in this area.

I am using the term conversion to indicate a genuine, integral, personal transformation. This conversion begins with our perspective, attitude, and thoughts and then moves to words, actions, and behaviors.

The goal for this chapter is to broaden our perspective by reflecting on how our thoughts and beliefs (character, attitude, and self-image) influence our behavior, and more importantly, how they can be improved. By working to enhance these elements consciously, we will strengthen our communication skills and reinforce our sense of identity. I hope to convey the idea that a complete transformation will move most of us away from agreeing with basal flight or fight. Instead we will become understanding and considerate problem solvers. A personal conversion of our mentality and identity will produce entirely new outcomes in our life.

In his book, *Self Matters,* Dr. Phil reveals how the constant conflicts and behaviors we have in our life - in particular, those that cause issues for us - have roots in deep convictions, and stories we believe about ourselves.[1]

These stories, or thoughts that underlie our behavior, are revealed by the things we tell ourselves in our mind (consciously, or unconsciously) and often even out loud. Dr. Phil calls these "tapes", and they are also known commonly as "life scripts."[2]

Confronting yourself, or holding yourself accountable for things you think or say is a part of this conversion process. We sometimes tell ourselves things that are not true. Confronting these false scripts means actively facing what we believe and working to change those beliefs that are untrue, because they are detrimental to our progress, regardless of how comfortable we are with them.

Change of this magnitude can be a moment of epiphany at times, or a work of slow progress at others. However, even accepting the most minute internal changes can have an exponential impact on us externally.

John had always strived for success, yet had a fear of fame. Realizing that these two ideas were often at odds, he asked himself why he was so concerned with being inconspicuous, even when it was impractical as a gifted speaker and influencer. The answer came from childhood experiences. In the instances where he received the most public exposure, the result was mistreatment by peers. Regardless of the reasons for their belittlement and rejection, the hurt that resulted created a desire to be anonymous.

John's parents often showed love by recognizing his achievements. On the one hand, John felt valued by this, yet on the other hand, he experienced jealousy and rejection by peers following the public recognition that sometimes ensued as a result. John was uncomfortable with exposure because of this and became conflicted. Every time he was on the cusp of success, he would find a way to self-sabotage. He says no to challenging or high profile projects at work because he tells himself, "People like me better when I am behind the scenes, and I am happier that way." Nothing could be further from the truth, however. First, he is not happy because he is not using his full abilities, and second, others wonder why he is always holding back or, despite obvious talent, fails to engage.

In John's case, the truth is that there will always be those who can't stand your success, but that shouldn't stop you from pursuing success. Being singled out is part of success, and only those who understand that the benefits of success outweigh the negatives will be able to move ahead without fear. Behaviors that may have been common in an elementary, or middle school setting should not be transferred into the corporate world. Unfortunately, jealousy and immaturity do exist even among adults, but that is not a reason to live life in a cocoon.

Whether you are on a quest for personal improvement or just want to get better at confrontation, dealing with scripts like John's is key to having lasting change. Ultimately, much of what we can do to better how we communicate and live comes down to this conversion.

Personal transformation also means addressing and building our character. Our character is based on values that we live by. By crystalizing our values, we can better live according to our beliefs about right and wrong. Our self concept and self-image is built on assumptions about our self and determines our behavior.[3] By consciously reviewing and affirming realistic and positive beliefs, we can improve this image of ourselves. It is by aligning our actions with our beliefs that we strengthen this image. How we see ourselves and what is important to us are not just factors in our behavior; they are the very foundation of how we act and live.

Our self-image and beliefs determine why we do what we do.

Nathanial Hawthorne said: "You cannot be one kind of person and another kind of performer and get by with it. You ultimately become confused as to who you are and your effectiveness is dramatically reduced."

What you do stems from who you are, and the two must agree. If you say that you are trustworthy, but tell a lie, then you have conflict. If you say that you love someone but don't make that person a priority, you are conflicted. If you say that you are a good runner, but you fail to practice and perform poorly in a race, you are conflicted. You cannot live life as a theory. There must be some external evidence that we are who we claim to be. Your actions will testify to who you are.

CHARACTER

One element of our selfhood is our character. It is a part of our identity, personality, and self-image. What is character?

Character refers to the mental and moral qualities distinctive to an individual: running away was not in keeping with her character.• the distinctive nature of something: gas lamps give the area its character.• the quality of being individual, typically in an interesting or unusual way: the island is full of character.• strength and originality in a person's nature: she had character as well as beauty.• a person's good reputation: to what do I owe this attack on my character?• dated a written statement of someone's good qualities; a recommendation.[4]

So then, character is personal, it has a lot to do with moral qualities, how strong or durable they are, and how apparent they are. The underlying mental aspects, or the personal thoughts we adhere to determine it.

And what is the impact of these character-defining thoughts? They give us our motivation for action. They determine what we do in a given situation and how we respond to others. By confronting character issues, we can become individuals of integrity, and learn to handle confrontation better. We will make better decisions and have fewer problems in life.

Our thoughts about our character motivate our actions.

So where do we get it and how is it improved? Character is developed and shaping it is a lifelong task. It comes from the Greek word kharakter, meaning "to engrave with a stick", or to mark permanently. Your deeply held beliefs about what is right and wrong, how you should treat others, and who you are, have all been impressed upon you at various points in your life through examples, teaching, and experiences.

Experiences and influences have engraved ideas and ideals upon your heart and mind. Some would also argue that natural law exists in the spirit. This natural law is an internal compass or inner voice of conscience that can often let us know when our chosen thoughts and actions are not in harmony with the direction we should take. This concept has given rise to what is commonly known as "true north" in popular media. True north is your internal desire to do what is right regardless of what is acceptable in today's society. Regardless of what people condone, your heart may not agree.

The character we live by is a choice.

The character you live by is a choice. You can choose to be punctual. When I was overweight, I one day made a decision that I could not live the same way. I then made choices about how I would change my life. I started with foods I decided I would no longer eat. By sticking to those choices and refining those goals I have improved my health. All of these choices point to a change or decision of character as well as action. I became a conscientious eater. Conscientious is the character element that describes my eating today.

How do we identify the character we want and develop it?

Think of some people that you respect, more specifically people who you think exhibit desirable character traits. Could you name those traits? The qualities that appeal to us may differ depending on who comes to mind. Observing those with upright character helps us identify who we want to be. Since you cannot be anyone else, we are talking about the old cliche, "becoming the best version of you." You must decide who you want to be. I am guessing if you are reading this book, then you likely want to be a more effective communicator, more confident, tactful, assertive, kind, patient, and responsible all as a minimum.

If you listed out all these notable character traits that come to mind, what would they be? Here is a list to get you started:

Punctual
Direct, a straight shooter
Good Natured
Sense of Humor
Honest and Truthful, a person of Integrity
Committed
Diligent, Persevering, Tenacious, Enduring
Humble
Meek
Teachable
Courageous
Thoughtful, Sensitive
Loving
Optimistic, Positive
Upbeat, Energetic
Loyal
Upright, Blameless
Calm, Cool, and Collected
Consistently employed and working towards something
Keeping commitments: doing what you say (*hint*, don't overcommit)

Once you identify these traits, you need to draw a correlation between what behavior exemplifies or demonstrates those qualities. That list could look like this:

1. Patience = not talking over others, listening until your turn, not fidgeting when in a line or waiting room, keeping your cool when unexpected and unavoidable delays arise.

2. Kindness = not saying things that demean (no name calling), using care with words and how you treat others.

3. Upright - following the rules, not doing anything evil, not saying anything evil.

If people are upset with you because you are always late, then you should address your view of punctuality and why you are deciding not to be on time. Is being tardy worth the constant negative consequences, and does it make you feel good? If you were always on time, how would it affect you? Perhaps you say that it is impossible to be on time all of the time. While there are times that circumstances change your plans, this should be the rare exception and not the rule. When you are always on time, people will understand the one time you have some real issue. Being late affects every area of a person's life and sends a signal that you do not value the time of others. Many people take your lack of care for their time as a sign that you do not value them. Tardiness ruins both relationships and career.

ATTITUDE

Attitude is a settled way of thinking or feeling about someone or something and typically reflected in a person's behavior. It is also a perspective, or thoughts and viewpoint on something. Personal transformation begins with our viewpoint and extends to words and actions. How we view things is the way we think. Famed cognitive psychologist, Martin Seligman, states 'One of the most significant findings in psychology in the last twenty years is that individuals can choose the way they think,.'[5]

We get to choose our thoughts.

We can change our perspective from one of inability, or "I can't," to one of ability, or "I Can." We can shift from a negative attitude to a positive attitude. We can decide to change from "I can't stand that person," to "I am learning how to work with that person." We can shift from, "I am so bad at confrontation and expressing myself" to "I am learning to express myself and deal with others." Attitude is our posture, meaning that we take a stance or position of readiness to do something.

Attitude is also defined as:
A position of the body proper to or implying an action or mental state: the boy was standing in an attitude of despair, his chin sunk on his chest.
Uncooperative behavior; or a resentful or antagonistic manner: "I asked the waiter for a clean fork, and all I got was attitude."
Informal individuality and self-confidence as manifested by behavior or appearance; style: she snapped her fingers with attitude.

Even more than this, attitude is the spirit with which we do something. It is the essence of the action.

It is said; Attitude determines altitude. How high or far you will go in life is based on your perspective and how you position yourself. You ready yourself for success with your thoughts, mood, self-presentation, and tendencies; by having the right attitude.

Our attitude towards others dictates how we treat others. We must examine it.

Let's start by agreeing that we want to be tactful, respectful, and genuine in our communication. Moreover, we desire to choose our words, tone, and expressions carefully and professionally, delivering them with kindness and consideration.

Shift Your Thoughts

Now we understand how thinking affects us, and that we can change it. What are some of the shifts we must make in our thinking to be successful in our relationships with others?

- Managing the negative feelings we have for others based on their shortcomings.

What this means is understanding that people are not only human and not only capable of mistakes, but prone to make them. Because of this inherent weakness, we should have some compassion and understanding because we too are human and also make mistakes. Often we don't realize the things that we do and the repercussions of them on others. So how should we deal with those that we work with, live with, and share space with, especially those that have negative behaviors?

- Learn to love the person and yet hate negative behavior.

We can choose to become people of peace, patience, and self-control. We can also grow in kindness, consideration, and empathy. We have the ability to become more self-aware as well as perceptive and sensitive to the feelings of others. Self-aware means we must become aware of our emotions, our behaviors and the consequences of those behaviors. It is possible to be both confident and assertive while remaining calm and humble.

- Becoming Socially Aware.

What does it take to become socially aware? Social awareness requires us looking for and noticing the comfort cues of others around us. How is the social setting and communication affecting their behavior, demeanor, and posture? Do they seem nervous, flustered, or upset? Are they red in the face, breathing heavy, or lifeless and staring down at the floor? These clues typically reveal the emotional and mental impacts of the social circumstance on the person. To the extent that we can do this, we can respond in a way that is both socially appropriate and doesn't undermine the point of our communication and relationships. The more subtle the cue, the more discerning we need to be.

Perhaps our intent is to help someone, but the way we do it is indiscriminate or careless, and then it backfires. Numerous examples come to mind. If you are trying to point out something to someone about their clothing but it is done in a way that embarrasses them or makes them uncomfortable, you defeat the purpose of trying to help them. Jane has a piece of paper or lint stuck to her hair. Instead of loudly saying, "What is going on with your hair? What is that?" you could try, instead, pulling her aside or simply leaning in, to say, "I just want to let you know it looks like there is something in your hair." Awareness of the individual's personality and picking up on comfort cues is critical because while some people may not be offended by anything, others are easily offended. Being thoughtfully caring, conscientious and discriminate are all displayed by doing this simple thing correctly.

Expect to be Challenged - Situational Antagonists (Triggers)

Today we are continually hearing about triggers in the field of coaching, academia, and in general. Triggers can be positive as illustrated in the coaching industry, where you can set up reminders or make preparations for challenging tasks in advance so that they trigger the positive response that you set out to achieve. However, more relevant to this section is the idea of a trigger as something that upsets you, sometimes without any relevance to the person who may accidentally set you off. It may be intended as some lighthearted joke or an honest suggestion, but because of past conditioning, we flip out and go berserk. Now if I say, "I am a kind, compassionate, and accepting individual," and then turn around and jump all over someone who has unintentionally rubbed me the wrong way, I have (been challenged and) failed to act consistently with my envisioned character.

Remember: "You cannot be one kind of person and another kind of performer and get by with it. You ultimately become confused as to who you are and your effectiveness is dramatically reduced." There is no way to separate your character from your behavior. Your behavior is what demonstrates your identity. Difficulties, temptations, and people test our virtue. Situational antagonists could include a long line at the checkout with a slow-moving cashier, and be compounded by the person in front of you who waited 20 minutes in line and still doesn't know what they want at the register. All of a sudden, you are irritated, and the slightest thing could cause an outburst. Or it could be the rudeness of someone else, who has decided that they are having a bad day. How we deal with these situational antagonists reveals our character. The less our behavior (actions or reactions) is changed or affected by situational antagonists, the stronger our moral mettle.

Situational antagonists are those factors with the potential to alter your behavior by applying momentary pressure.

If you walk into a room and someone you know says, "hey beautiful" or "hey stupid," how do you respond? If you walk into a room and a stranger says the same, how do you respond? If you walk into a room and accidentally bump into someone, who says, "hey idiot, watch where you are going," how do you respond? Character is tested every day by antagonistic factors. It is how we react to these factors that separate the common from the great. In no place is this more evident than our communication with others.

When the worst has been brought out of us by unusual circumstances, we should evaluate whether our response was appropriate and how to temper or calm our behavior next time. Yes, we are all human, but that doesn't give us the right to act without restraint, or heaven forbid, like animals.

Character that passes testing is strengthened.
Building character means not only how we act but how we respond to situations. Critically what this means is learning how to handle trying or uncomfortable situations.

Deciding In Advance

A person of character should learn to recognize and anticipate challenging moments. If you know what sets you off, then when it happens you can tell yourself, "stop, breathe, and don't take the bait." In other words, don't give in to the temptation to get upset. Preparing for these moments is done by understanding what you would regret doing, or not doing, and making a decision that if you are ever faced with this situation, here is how you will respond. Deciding in advance sets you up to overcome temptation. What does this look like? It can be as simple making a list of I will's and I will not's. That list can look like this:

I will not yell when upset

I refuse to swear

I will follow the law at all times

I will call a timeout when frustrated, angry, or unsure of how to handle myself in a given situation

I will not hit others or engage in any physical altercation unless defending my life or the lives of others (and only when there are no other options)

I will not litter

I will take my trash out of the car and dispose of it every time I exit the vehicle.

I will go to bed on time, so I can get a good night's sleep and be refreshed

I will not entertain or solicit the improper advances of others

I will respect my marriage by, x,y,z

I will not make impulse buys

I will stick to my budget

Role-Playing

Role-Playing can also add another dimension to this preparation. Role-playing is where one or more people act out a role or character. They pretend to be someone else or play a role in a fictitious story. Like improvisation, they make choices and dialog as they go. For our purposes of engaging in character development, those role-playing may pretend to be a character (or themselves in a theoretical scenario), while in this instance you remain as yourself.

Role-playing serves as the flight simulation of challenging conversations. One person will play the antagonist. Examples relative to confrontation could be responding to someone who is upset, fanatical, or accusatory. You will play yourself and try to best react to their difficult behavior without getting upset or violating your character. Exercises like this can help you prepare for real tests and think through how you might respond. It will also help to train you to think before you answer, learning to pause before answering.

Changing Your Character (Recognizing the Need)

When a person is continually aloof, rude, or sarcastic, it may not be so easy to change, and so we must first realize and recognize the behavior. The famous Jack Handey story goes like this: People were always talking about how mean this guy was who lived on our block. But I decided to go see for myself. I went to his door, but he said he wasn't the mean guy, the mean guy lived in that house over there. "No, you stupid idiot," I said, "that's my house."[6]

The first part of this conversion process is awareness. Until we recognize that we need change (and the areas where we need it), we cannot adequately address it. By role-playing or even paying more attention to the things you say, you might learn that surprising things are coming out of your mouth and you don't even realize it. You may have become desensitized to your behavior patterns.

The second part is to believe that you can change. There is hope. Millions of people have lost weight, found a mate, started a new career, and improved their communication skills. Dr. John Maxwell says, "If there's hope in the future, there's power in the present."[7] The idea is that where there is hope, there is motivating energy, and there is action. If it can work for others, it can work for you too. The difference in success is in the system and principles used, and not the individual. Apply the principles, work the system, and you will see progress.

The third part is to understand the impact of the words we speak. Begin to think about what we are saying. In other words, what do the words mean? How will those words be received? How does it sound? The words we use and the thoughts that they invoke drive our happiness, success, and fulfillment, or hopelessness and frustration. Science now shows how words impact the brain for better or worse.[8] Imagine if the things you say would happen just by your speaking them out loud. It is not that far from reality. When someone repeatedly is told that they are stupid, it is quite likely they will eventually begin to believe it and act stupidly. Name-calling is one of the worst behaviors, and not the way to treat others. It is one that we should all strive to eliminate from our lives. For every time you are tempted to say something terrible about someone, try to think the opposite and say something nice about them instead. The process of taking control of one's tongue takes a conscious effort but will make us and everyone around us better off.

Words shape the self-esteem and images we have of ourselves and others, particularly at a young age. As we grow, we can choose to take an active role if we understand this principle. When dealing with others, we must be considerate of their personhood - it's their self-esteem and more. That means having compassion in our delivery of feedback and working to deliver our content in a way that they can receive.

In our personal life, we also need to deal with ourselves similarly, with compassion and realism. Beating yourself up over things rarely produces excellent results. Instead, resolve to do things differently.

The fourth part is understanding the source of inputs in our life.

Friends, family, and associations. Those we surround ourselves with are a major part of who we are and who we become. If you are not surrounding yourself with positive people, it may be time to make some new acquaintances.

Media. The books you read, the shows you watch, and the music you listen to, all have an impact on your behavior. Thought polarization is the term given to the outcome of dwelling on something incessantly. In psychology, this principle states that always thinking about an issue tends to produce more extreme, resistant attitudes.

Thinking doesn't make you an extremist, but continually thinking about the same thing in the same way repeatedly may ultimately make you an extremist.[9]

You can be extremely positive and optimistic, or extraordinarily cynical and pessimistic. The media, mainly the news, can cause us to become hyper-aware of situations that have a negative impact on our perspective and outlook on life.

Add to your character list what kind of books the person you want to be like reads. What kind of shows do they watch or not watch? Movies? Websites? Social Media?

There is a Cherokee Legend, called The Wolves Within, that illustrates this point. In the legend, an old Cherokee is teaching his grandson about life. "A fight is going on inside me," he said to the boy. "It is a terrible fight, and it is between two wolves. One is evil - he is anger, envy, sorrow, regret, greed, arrogance, self-pity, guilt, resentment, inferiority, lies, false pride, superiority, and ego." He continued, "The other is good - he is joy, peace, love, hope, serenity, humility, kindness, benevolence, empathy, generosity, truth, compassion, and faith. The same fight is going on inside you - and inside every other person, too." The grandson thought about it for a minute and then asked his grandfather, "Which wolf will win?" The old Cherokee simply replied, "The one you feed." [10]

You have two identities inside of you. The one you truly desire to be, and the one you fear yourself to be. The one you fuel will dominate. You must feed yourself with noble thoughts, good media, and the right influences to have a healthy self-identity.

Another adaptation of this same story called Grandfather Tells puts it this way: A young man came to his grandfather and shared how he was angry at a friend who had done him an injustice. "Let me tell you a story. I too, at times, have felt a great hate for those that have taken so much, with no sorrow for what they do. But hate wears you down and does not hurt your enemy. It is like taking poison and wishing your enemy would die. I have struggled with these feelings many times." He continued, "It is as if there are two wolves inside me. One is good and does not harm others. He lives in harmony with all around him and does not take offense when no offense was intended. He will only fight when it is right to do so and in the right way. But the other wolf, ah! He is full of anger. The littlest thing will set him into a fit of temper. He fights everyone, all the time, for no reason. He cannot think because his anger and hate are so intense. It is helpless anger, for his anger will change nothing. Sometimes, it is hard to live with these two wolves inside me, for both of them try to dominate my spirit." The boy looked intently into his grandfather's eyes and asked, "Which one wins, Grandfather?" The grandfather smiled and quietly said, "The one I feed."[11]

I include this second adaptation because it points to several additional ideas. The first is that anger becomes hate when it is held onto. Anger often can blind us to the truth, and prevent us from thinking clearly. Also as it highlights, often this anger is to no avail. Indeed it will harm us. Finally, there is the idea that these emotions can take over and dominate our spirit if we are not careful. Our identity is at stake when it comes to ruling over our feelings.

So how can we feed the good wolf? How can we strengthen ourselves spiritually to live in harmony, love, joy, and peace? We must feed on the right food. We must feed ourselves with books, stories, and teachings that focus on, create a sense of, and empower us to live in this way. We must have an ongoing relationship with those who exemplify these powerfully positive and spiritually purifying qualities.

We need to change the inputs in our lives to change our outlook on life. We must change our outlook on life if we want to improve our output, or what we produce and accomplish in our daily lives. The adage, you are what you eat, is also true regarding thought consumption. We consume thoughts from the media we follow, the conversations we have, and the experiences we allow. The people around us, in part, create some of those experiences. You may need to evaluate and to make the necessary changes concerning the people you surround yourself with, your media consumption, and your speech if you want to make a lasting difference in your life. The constant or regular company of dysfunctional people can become a breeding ground for dysfunction, or emotional and spiritual sickness. The proverbs of ancient times remind us:

Keep company with the wise and you will become wise. If you make friends with stupid people, you will be ruined.

and also,

Don't make friends with anyone who has a bad temper. You might learn their habits and not be able to change.

We must keep company with those that understand, agree, and strive to live to the same moral standards to which we adhere, and even at a higher level. It is those who live to a higher moral standard that can help to elevate us.

High moral standards are those that consider others and the integrity of self.

Psychiatrist Max Levine said: "There cannot be emotional health in the absence of high moral standards and a sense of social responsibility." It all goes together. If you want to be emotionally healthy, you must strive to live to the standard of your beliefs about what is right.[12]

SELF-ESTEEM & SELF IMAGE

How do you currently show that you value yourself? Others? What we value we protect, nurture, invest in, and work toward improving. We treat the things we value with care. The proof that you appreciate someone is revealed by how you treat them.

Our first step to treating others well is to love ourselves. If you can't value yourself, you will have a hard time appreciating anyone else. You must know that you are valuable. An understanding of our full value is found in our uniqueness as well as our purpose. When we find a way to benefit others and fulfill a role in society, we see our lives as both valuable and meaningful. When you contribute (as only you can) to the common good and causes that are more significant than your own life, you find fulfillment and satisfaction. Self-satisfaction comes by adding to the satisfaction of others. Contributing to others gives us meaning. It provides us with a sense of worth.

As stated, part of your value is locked in your purpose. Identifying and living for it will add meaning to your life. Knowing "what you were created to do," is linked with increased happiness, more energy, and better outcomes in life.[15]

There are many resources that can help you discover your purpose. Start by asking yourself, "What things have meaning to me?"

Not sure you qualify? Everything and everyone has a purpose and a place in the world. We can see this demonstrated on many levels in nature, the food chain, and life in general. For instance, kelp exists to create food and habitat for not only sea creatures but also for humans. In Australia alone, it is estimated that industries supported by kelp bring billions of dollars of value.[13] Numerous sea creatures and ecosystems could not exist apart from kelp. If a leafy green seaweed has a mission so vital, then how can you not be more valuable? In fact, no two people are the same, each of us is unique, wonderful, and capable of adding something to the world. There is the first key! It is putting our focus on adding, creating, serving, helping, and doing something good for others. While you may not have fully discovered your purpose, that in no way disproves its existence.

Imagine using a priceless artifact of ancient pottery for an ashtray. Better still, imagine using a cell phone as a hammer. It seems funny to us because we know the intended use of the cell phone. However, in the hands of a cave man, it could easily be used for a hammer because of a lack of knowledge and understanding. To know how to use something correctly, you need the manual. You need training and input from others with experience. Reading great books allows us to learn more about life from those who have already been on ahead of us. These works can serve as a manual for life. We can discover how to live meaningful lives. Purpose and value go hand in hand with the way we treat others and live. When we don't understand the use of something, we misuse it or misappropriate it. When we value others, we treat them appropriately. Valuing ourselves and valuing others are inextricably linked.

Here are some more questions to help you think about your purpose:

What excites you? What angers you?
What dominates your thoughts? What keeps you up at night?
What do others say about you?
What comes quickly to you, and what is difficult?
You have just been given 100 Million Dollars, what would you do with the rest of your life?

Answering these questions should help you get started.

The key to life is effective communication. The key to communication is listening. Listening is made easy by asking the right questions in the right way. You must ask yourself the right questions so that you can hear from your heart. Many people go traveling trying to find themselves when they just need to get to know themselves. Knowing yourself, finding your purpose, and unlocking your value all cause you to build a valuable resource known as confidence.

Confidence is your greatest asset in life. If you have value, then shouldn't you take care of yourself? If you have value, then don't others? You can't help others if you can't function. Take care of your self so that you can be and do your best at all times. Take care of your self so that you can help others.

Belief in something prepares you to act because it gives you a reason (why). The answer to why we should do something provides us with an idea to refer to when the going is tough. It anchors our decision and informs our actions. When you answer the "why" question, you have principles. When you act according to your beliefs, you get the rewards; one of them is always self-esteem, and the other is integrity. The prize for keeping your word is trust. Believing that truthfulness in your words is the only way to live is what will cause you to keep your word. Being trustworthy enables others to commit things like information, relationship, responsibility, and authority to you. The pattern in life is that first you will be tested with small things, and once you have proven to be faithful with those, more responsibility, authority, and greater financial benefits will flow to you like a river. You must believe that truthfulness matters.

The New You: Building Character and Developing a Healthy Personality

People can change. It requires some work, and it will require continual self-assessment. Many people avoid self-assessment at all costs, while super achievers are not only more aware but they invite critique, seek mentorships and coaching and invest in themselves. Super achievers are those people that achieve more than others. They continually strive for successive achievements and develop behaviors that allow them to overcome every obstacle to their desired goals and outcomes. They also happen to have a healthy self-image that can weather setbacks, failures, and defeats.

Developing a Healthy Personality

How would we describe this healthy personality?

1. Flexible and compromising, looking for successful communication strategies
2. Able to cope with and deal with loss, failure, or disappointment.
3. Positive thinking, outlook, and attitude
4. Ability to reflect on your behavior
5. Work on empathizing with others - learn to listen
6. Avoid blaming others, gossip, and put-downs
7. Be an encourager, good finder
8. Accepting responsibility for behaviors as well as problems and solving them

To become emotionally healthy you must deal with negatives and overcome them.

Chief among the negatives that we must deal with are the negative thoughts we have about ourself. *Basing your self-worth off of how others treat you is a mistake!* Instead, base your self-esteem off of a healthy ideal image of yourself.

Even if you are not fully living according to that image, believe that this "ideal you" is alive inside of you and must be drawn out. To draw that potential out we must focus on it and strengthen it. We can affirm that image with our attitude and outlook, words and appearance, and by our actions in private and public. We can also strengthen it by valuing others and demonstrating that value in how we treat them, their interests, and their property.

Your healthy self-image is based upon a picture of yourself that you hold in your mind and heart. It is who you believe yourself to be (or will become). Your positive identity encompasses you morally and ethically, emotionally, mentally, spiritually, physically and socially.

WHY WE ARE THE WAY WE ARE
(AND WHY KNOWING WHY IS NOT ENOUGH)

Memories & Wounds

Remember we discussed how those emotionally significant events in your life created memories? Some of these were negative, some positive, and still others have a mix of both. Those memories are tied to convictions and feelings. The negative patterns and feelings exist as long as the beliefs live on in our mind. We cannot change the memories, but we can change the views we developed as a result, as well as the emotions we experience when we remember them.

Manipulation of memories to change facts is deceitful at best. We should not attempt to rewrite what happened. However, we can replace the feelings tied to the event. We can change the way we feel about the evidence. The facts, in this case, are things that happened, not necessarily what we perceived happened. The best way to change our feelings about the past is to re-examine the evidence. When we cast new light on the facts, or introduce new evidence, then new verdicts can be made about the events. These new verdicts and conclusions supersede (replace or overwrite) the old, and bring relief from the problems created by the former. The one who is being found innocent by the judgment, in this case, is you. Those enslaving beliefs from the memories were like a prison keeping you bound, and their bondages can now be destroyed, effectively setting you free. Where you have blamed yourself you unjustly, you can now remove blame for what went wrong.

What about cases where you cannot excuse yourself from blame? Forgive yourself. No sense in beating yourself up. No matter how grave the error, or how awful the mistake. Every day you spend living with guilt you rob society of your full potential. You deprive others of the opportunity to give you another chance. You cheat yourself the benefits of living free from shame. It is time to move on and forgive yourself. Let me repeat it; *it is time.*

Liberating experiences (which create new memories) are waiting. Make these experiences the kind that affirm your core beliefs and solidify your ideal self-image. An example of this is a person with a fear of heights. Perhaps they fell from a chair as a child or maybe saw a movie where someone fell. Science shows that both could have the same impression on a child. A liberating new experience is climbing a mountain or high building. Doing this without falling destroys the belief that they will fall. They conquer their fear of heights with this experience.

What if someone else is to blame for the facts?

FORGIVENESS

Forgiveness is a decision.

Forgiveness can often seem challenging, especially forgiving when we feel upset or hurt by someone. However, *that is why we need to forgive in the first place!* We are the ones who suffer the most by holding un-forgiveness - which causes us to become bitter, or insensitive to others, (and not just those that hurt us).

The good news is that while you may not feel like forgiving the person, forgiveness doesn't require feelings to be successful. It only needs you to decide to forgive them.[16] I am guessing you have probably apologized for something before. The same way that perhaps someone else has pardoned you, you can also forgive others. You did not have to feel forgiven to confess and apologize, but for sure you probably did after! Forgiving others is the same; you have the feeling of relief after, not before.

To forgive, we must first decide to do so and believe that it is a matter of saying it out loud. To the offender, if they are alive, but if not then out loud to yourself. The same way we received forgiveness by confessing to others, we must believe that we have the power to forgive that person and then speak it.

If you need to forgive someone, you must decide that you will do it, and then say it out loud, even speaking to the person as though they were in front of you, "So and so, I forgive you for XYZ." You will begin to feel differently after, although it may be instant, it may not. Calling or speaking to them in person is preferred, but not always practical or possible.

You can even forgive yourself in this same way. Say, "Self, I forgive you for such and such," (or insert your name), and in turn, accept the apology.

Sometimes it helps to understand that the person who hurt us is also a victim of sorts or has slipped up (and possibly too ashamed or proud to admit it). We are all subject to weakness. Quite often people don't realize the extent of their words or actions, or in some cases are clueless to the fact they did something wrong. This is the sad state of the world. We need to have compassion for others and to sympathize with them as we have also done wrong without realizing or wanting to. We don't forgive others because they are good, but instead, we forgive them because they did something wrong. You only need to forgive someone if they did something wrong. We also forgive others because we have done wrong in the past and certainly will likely blow it at some point again. Finally, we forgive others because it is the right thing to do. For our health, and for our conscience.

Refusing to forgive someone is like drinking poison and expecting the other person to get sick.

When you hold a grudge, the negative emotions that you experience are a stress response taking place in your brain, with the release of cortisol.[17] As mentioned earlier in this book, stress can have devastating health consequences. When you forgive someone, however, your brain releases oxytocin. This love hormone is a potent antidepressant that not only helps you feel good but improves your life. While you are busy fuming over their actions, they are going on in life. You are losing time, energy, and focus obsessing over their deeds. Save yourself the trouble and get over it by forgiving them. Even better, do it to their face and explain why you are upset in the first place.

But you don't know what they did to me! How can I just let it go? Often people want to see someone destroyed for something they have done to them. So often people judge others harshly for that which they also practice. When we fail to separate people from their behavior, we put ourselves in danger of not only becoming bitter, callous and unforgiving but also hypocritical. I have yet to meet a person who has never offended someone. Perhaps you are always perfect and have never made a mistake in your life? Don't be guilty of a double standard of judgment. That is when you measure others on a different scale than yourself. Most often this is seen when we judge ourselves by our intentions and others by their actions.

Some people say *forgive but don't forget*. While we don't necessarily mean you should deny the incident ever happened, you should not hold it over their heads as extortion, as that is not forgiving it at all. If the person is a career offender, then we should carefully consider how much we will trust them. Trust is earned. Forgiveness is given. These are two different things. You can forgive someone without giving them carte blanche trust. Use some wisdom.

Others still don't believe it is necessary to forgive others directly, whether to their face or on the phone. This attitude also may assume that you can or should forgive without confronting the person and without confronting the behavior. The other reality is that this misses the opportunity to help the person and also to make them aware that their actions were unacceptable. By clearly identifying that boundary and how the behavior crossed it, you have the opportunity to both create new ways of interaction for yourself and the individual. For you this means:

You will have gained the respect of the person.
You will have prevented fear, isolation, and the risk of not having dealt with the situation from creating a negative perspective.
You will prevent the forming of walls and barriers between yourself and others, especially that person.
You maintain your freedom of expression and the right to be heard.
You hone your communication skills and improve your chances of success, positive impact, and greatness.
You groom yourself for leadership and management.

You distinguish yourself from others who fail to communicate.

For the other person:

You make them aware of their behavior and its consequence.
You give them an opportunity to correct the situation.
You provide them with a chance to explain and/or apologize - perhaps that is not what they meant or intended (by what they said in the first place).
You give them an opportunity for healing - perhaps they are dealing with significant issues and feel isolated, hurt and are just reacting out of frustration with their life.
You give them an opportunity to change the way they communicate, live, and behave.
You give them a second chance at life that they would not otherwise have received. If every person just said to themselves, "Well, I am going to let go of what they did but cut them off," how will this person ever change?

Hurt people hurt people, but what the world needs is menders. Go ahead and mend the relationship.

Every time someone wrongs us, we have the opportunity to choose how we will respond. Painful emotions and memories (experienced as a result of that moment) can be accumulated or avoided depending on our perspective and reaction to the perceived offense. When we confront the issue and the person with a successful outcome, we can conquer any feelings of affront. The best way to do this is to thoughtfully communicate with honesty what our interpretation of their actions means to us. On the other hand, if we keep silent and avoid saying anything to the person about the situation, we create a state of aversion to them. This avoidance can become an aversion to speaking up and interacting with others in general. This is because the wounded often build walls to protect themselves from the outside world. Checking or guarding ourselves by restricting open engagement with others is done to prevent us from being hurt. Because of this fear of being hurt again, they feel that the cannot show their authentic self. Perhaps some people are comfortable sharing things over social media because it allows them to seethe when offended and, if desired, cut off the relationship. Maybe they feel safer because they are not in the presence of the person on the other side of the social media post. Rejections have caused people to seek acceptance with endless selfies and other attempts at belonging and getting praise. Sharing your life with the public doesn't necessarily make for intimate and meaningful relationships, but oftentimes, rather shallow, hollow, and "built for display" lifestyles.

EMOTIONAL SECURITY

Security: the state of feeling safe, stable, and free from fear or anxiety: this man could give the emotional security she needed.
Origin: late Middle English: from Old French "securite" or Latin "securitas," from "securus," 'free from care' (see secure).

Security blanket: |sə'kyo͞orədē 'blaNGkət|noun1) a familiar blanket or other piece of soft fabric held by a young child as a source of

```
comfort. Something that provides reassurance,
support, or a sense of security: investors no
longer see gold as a security blanket.
```

Emotional security is affected by our surroundings and can be damaged through traumatic events, especially when these events happen at a young age. It is our rational conclusions about these events that become ingrained beliefs, which affect our self-image, self-esteem, and our sense of worth and ability. Theories that we develop in response to traumatic experiences can be labeled traumatic beliefs. Called maladaptive beliefs, they are often disempowering and painful, and they beget emotional wounds. Emotional wounds are resulting emotions that are tied to the beliefs we created as a result of the traumatic experience.

Too often people seek to heal the original traumatic experience and not the post-traumatic belief. In most cases, this approach is difficult or impossible. When we realize that the post-traumatic beliefs that we hold about ourselves and the world are the actual emotional wounds, then we can heal by correcting those beliefs. We fix or replace those beliefs by changing the conclusion about the events or person's behavior.

For instance, a child blames him or herself for a parent's divorce, drinking, or leaving. A mother blames herself for the loss of a child. These create a multitude of issues. Forgiving one's self of any fault and releasing one's self from the responsibility of those outcomes is essential to becoming whole and emotionally healthy.

These false beliefs can create social needs. We try to meet those needs so that we can experience temporary security. Unfortunately, these false beliefs tend to create an invisible barrier that keeps the emotional need from being fulfilled. If you believe that you are not worthy, any affirmation of worth will only bring temporary relief or possibly be doubted entirely. The feeling of worthiness can't coexist with present beliefs about low self-worth. However, if you can change your beliefs about your self, you will resolve the conflict as well as the need for constant outside affirmation.

Healing can come with a realization of truth about one's self and a change of beliefs. First, you must realize that the idea is wrong and replace it with a new theory. An example mentioned earlier in this book was of a child's rejection by parents. The child thought he was no good as a result. To address this feeling, he continually sought approval to validate himself, yet to no avail. However, one day he realized that it was not him who had the issues, it was his parents. He realized that their behavior was not his fault. He no longer felt inadequate, inferior, or unlovable. He forgave his parents. Finally, he also concluded that he was lovable. This new belief also changed his self-image. Being able to receive the acceptance of those around him improved his actions towards them. He no longer needs to seek the approval of others for his security. Since he doesn't have to please everyone, he is also able to speak up for himself and has thereby reduced the conflicts he previously experienced. His communication is changed because he is changed. He has had a conversion of belief.

As we have seen in this chapter, if we want to confront external problems, we must first face internal conflicts and problems. Being able to confront others starts with you. The internal confrontation begins by dealing with personal fears, beliefs, and emotions. In the next chapter, we will look at ways to handle difficult conversations in the context of confronting others. In the meantime, focus on maintaining a positive attitude by reviewing the summary below.

WAYS TO MAINTAIN A POSITIVE ATTITUDE

Look for the good in every situation and every person, including yourself.

Be thankful for the good - millions of people have a gratitude journal or daily time to give thanks.

Act on your appreciation - small deeds make a big difference in how we feel.

Refuse to complain. Complaining can make you feel worse, won't move you closer to a solution, and can annoy others. It can seem selfish.

Reframe or label negative situations as opportunities (not problems) and look for solutions.

Believe in who you are becoming and your ability to live to your ideals. Focus on helping others.

Focus on how you will grow.

Celebrate successes.

Be generous with your kindness - with your words and deeds - to others and yourself.

Learn to forgive.

5

ABOUT THAT CONVERSATION: HOW SHOULD WE CONFRONT

This chapter is all about how to plan for and navigate a verbal confrontation or difficult conversation. Many of these points can apply to a broad range of important conversations as well. A difficult conversation can simply be defined as a conversation where one of the parties' comfort is uncertain due to the nature, topic, or timing of the conversation. It can be considered a confrontation when there is an element of accountability or sensitive issues to address. Some good examples of important conversations include big meetings, reviews, and difficult or pivotal conversations and interactions.

The goal in these conversations must become about confronting the issue, and not the person.

Use this chapter as a guide before and after these conversations. By coming back afterward, you can critique yourself for future improvement and be better prepared the next time around. Remember, this is a journey, not just a destination. You can review some of these points daily and weekly. Put them to use as you seek to improve your relationships at home and at work, and improve your effectiveness when addressing issues with others.

PLANNING FOR CONFRONTATION

Confrontation is to face something or someone head-on, or face to face, descending from the Latin words for *with* and *forehead,* or *face.* We can liken it to the terms *head on,* or *face to face.*[1]

Any time we are dealing with someone or something directly with an aim to bring change, we are confronting.

WHEN TO CONFRONT

I was angry with my friend: I told my wrath, my wrath did end. I was angry with my foe: I told it not, my wrath did grow.

William Blake

Don't delay!

Delaying a difficult conversation or action delays the benefits of solving the problem or issue, and continues the pains of it, often with complications and sometimes increased severity. Delay also creates an opportunity for:

Complaining.[2] Why put yourself in a situation where you can't get it off of your mind, or off of your chest. If you become miserable you will be challenged to conceal it, or worse, become a nuisance. Complaining happens when we see the problem but don't really see the solution, or worse; we see the solution but refuse to work towards it.

Backbiting/Gossip/Slander.[3] Backbiting, or talking about others behind their back (in a negative way) is wrong. Besides being unethical, it could be illegal. Defamation is a serious crime. A person's reputation should be among their most valuable possessions. A good name opens doors for someone, and a bad name shuts them. Talking about others even in frustration can hurt them in more ways than one. If you have an issue with someone, you need to tell them rather than talk about it with others. Should you destroy someone's life over a misunderstanding? If you make yourself the judge, jury, and execution squad without giving them a chance, you can be sure that there will be some negative consequences.

Seething.[4] Seething is when anger is kept alive internally. Your disgust for the person is increased by meditation on the offense. As discussed earlier, this can lead to passive-aggressive behavior. Seething causes anger to burn hot and spill over into yelling, name calling and unprofessional behavior. It can be misdirected at coworkers, family and friends who all may have nothing to do with the person you are really upset with. Anger is deadly. Anger causes physical stress on the body.

Reduced productivity.[5] *Personal stress and frustration* are not only an annoyance to others, they reduce your ability to do things well. Your ability to focus on the present task and do it well requires removing whatever is hanging over your head.

The conversation isn't going to get easier just because time has passed. The conversation only gets easier when you are prepared. Let's remind ourselves that problems don't just solve themselves.

Wait Just a Minute!

Now that you are in a hurry, hold on. Take a deep breath! How should we go about this? Just barrel in and spill our guts, whether good, bad and ugly? *Let's do this classy if possible, and prepared at worst.*

Vent on paper - You have got to get rid of the toxic emotions first. Venting on paper can greatly reduce emotional anxiety and help us reframe our thoughts.[7] We should never confront in anger, and you certainly don't want to blow your top and end up feeling worse afterwards. Writing a draft conversation or email is a powerful way to say what you would like to but won't. Hit delete and start fresh. Whether an email or a conversation, write or speak out several drafts as needed and then revise them, or trash them as appropriate.

Don't jump to conclusions without evidence - As you are planning and thinking, here is something to consider: It may not be what you think.[8] All too often we let fear or perception tell us that someone did something bad to us intentionally and we draw conclusions without investigation. Let's step back. Being falsely accused is awful to experience and unflattering to do. Often times we expect others to do the impossible without questioning our logic. Examples include assumptions about what we think others should know about us, like our opinions and feelings. "Didn't they think that I would be upset?" Surprisingly the answer is "no", and often with good reason.

Innocent until Proven Guilty - we are all prone to error, and often we judge harder than we should. Make sure you have the facts confirmed. Don't draw any conclusions until you have spoken to the person in question. Is it legal to convict a man before he is given a hearing? It must be innocent until proven guilty. A wise man once said,

> *Spouting off before listening to the facts*
> *is both shameful and foolish.*

> *and*

> *The first to speak in court sounds right - until the cross-examination begins. The one who states his case first seems right, until the other comes and examines him.*

Kindness, Gentleness, Mercy, Compassion - Gentleness doesn't imply weakness, but rather requires strength. Have mercy and compassion with your approach. You never know what they are going through behind the scenes. Perhaps something awful has happened to them, and no one knows about it. Whatever the case, don't dishonor yourself by letting yourself be unkind.

Mega famous performance coach Brendon Burchard tells the story of his plans to confront a celebrity client whom he refers to as Sandra in his book, *High Performance Habits.*[6] He has encouraged Sandra to be more courageous by posting real and vulnerable content on social media. When he receives a call from her at 2:47 AM, he watches her first video diary. Because the video seems shallow, he is unimpressed. Worse, she begins to panic about the negative comments, and she asks to meet with him right away. Feeling that she hasn't been that courageous, that the public reaction is trivial, he is just about to tell her why she is acting silly. It's then, when he is biting his tongue across from her in the back of a cafe, that he discovers why he is wrong. Beneath her dark sunglasses, she has a black eye and her significant other has been physically abusing her. It was her husband hitting her after seeing the video that really set her off. Of course, he instantly realizes that all of his assumptions and judgments are off, that Sandra is not overreacting and that she was being brave. The point of this illustration is that even a pro can be totally wrong in their conclusions about others. Brendon is one of the most recognized coaches in the world and yet allowed himself to jump to conclusions before the conversation even started. This example isn't to say anything negative about Brendon (as he held his tongue and asked all the right questions). It is to say that as humans, we make poor decisions when we don't have all the information.

Phased confrontation? There is always the possibility that you will need to ease into the discussion over a series of short conversations. That can be okay too. Set the stage and the wheels in motion. Introduce an issue or the fact that you have a problem. With shorter conversations, you will need to stick to a limited set of goals or goal and be focused. Sometimes change takes many small steps, often a series of acknowledgments or discussions.

HOW SHOULD WE CONFRONT?

Prepared - You need to make sure you know what you are going to say as well as how you will say it.

Ask yourself these questions:

What is the vision for the conversation? Picture how you would like it to go.

How do you want to appear, come off, and be remembered? The brilliance of your words is not as important as the attitude and manner in which you convey them. People are more likely to remember how your words and approach made them feel over and above the actual facts, or exact words spoken. How you make others feel is what they will remember. Your kindness (or lack thereof) will make more of an impression than your vocabulary or genius. You need to prepare your mind, heart, and attitude and align them with your vision for the conversation. Will you be at peace, calm, organized, thoughtful, forgiving, merciful, competent, patient? If so then you have to arrive at the correct *attitude* or *spirit* before you show up for the talk.

1. **Why are we having this conversation?** What happened that made this necessary? What is the mission of the conversation? What is the desired outcome? What do I hope to accomplish?

What would a win look like in this situation? Maybe it would be the other person accepting your apology, or listening to what you have to say. Perhaps it is getting them to admit how they feel. Maybe it is getting them to understand something important. You decide. You need to build your statements around the mission.

2. **What do I want to communicate to the person?** Is it to tell them "your attitude stinks," or "I need to know what you think here," or "I appreciate what you did"? If it is about something they did, then let them know what they did, how it made you feel and why it is an issue. Know what you are trying to get across. Take time to think through the situation and what the facts are.

3. **How will I say it?** Taking the time to simply phrase the words is the most important thing you can do alongside planning a strategy. Instead of saying, "you're a jerk," you can say, "I am feeling like you don't like me." If they ask why that is, don't say "you act like a jerk," try "based on your behavior."

How you say it includes not only what you say but your delivery, attitude, and mood. You want to be:

Calm. Make sure you get all of your frustration out. Go for a walk or a run, or hit the gym. Try to be at your best and at least make sure you won't be at your worst. Don't go hungry or tired or at the end of your day if you can avoid it. You are trying to relieve stress, not create it.

Attitude. Start in a spirit of gentleness. Yelling, grilling, and being accusatory will only put others on the defensive. Don't force them to justify their behavior by being aggressive. That will likely not achieve the results you really want. It is a natural human reaction to jump into a default strategy of self protection when you feel attacked. Use appeals as opposed to ultimatums. Ask and entreat instead of demanding. Use questions instead of statements.

The root causes of the issues will not be addressed unless the person feels safe enough to engage. You must go in to have a simple conversation focusing on truth. Remember we are here to get to the heart of the issue - that means telling the truth. Start with positives about the person or the job, relationship, etc. The positives are actually the reason we need to sort this out because we have something worth preserving. Admonish. Acknowledge the good and why this matters in the big picture. Be honest and sincere.

Listening - Give the other person a chance to speak. Try asking questions that will get them to think without being accusatory. Give them the freedom to talk, and affirm that you are paying attention. Short phrases or words such as,

"I see," "I hear you," "I understand," "OK, keep going," and "I'm listening," are all helpful when used appropriately. Eye contact (not glaring or staring), and nodding are also prime examples of positive listening feedback. This feedback reinforces the sense that you understand their point of view.

Questions can prompt or invite others to speak up during the discussion, and great ones make conversations easy. While too many inquiries have the potential to make someone feel uncomfortable, it is more important to consider what kind of questions you will ask as well as how you will ask them. How you ask sets the tone. The best way to find out what another person thinks, feels, or perceives is to ask. Let's remove any false assumptions we may have about a situation by politely asking.

Here are some examples:

How do you feel about the x, y, z decision today?
What are you feeling about x, y, z?
What did you think about x, y, z?
When did things start to really go wrong?
What was it that set you off?
What was it about that comment - what does that mean to you? To me I was trying to say, x, y, z.
Why didn't you come to me earlier?
Is something bothering you?

Hold Your Tongue - Listening will require giving others space to talk. You must also do your best to let others finish what they are saying (don't interrupt or cut others off). The worst thing you can do is ask another question or try to tell a story when someone isn't done sharing what could be important information. Knowing when to keep quiet is often more important than knowing what to say!

If you have been speaking for more than 3 minutes to answer a question, you might appear dominating or conversation hogging. Try to stick to only the issue at hand (not every issue ever) and please, no rabbit holes.

Remember to think before you speak. If the other person gets defensive or insults you, you must be ready and committed to not give in to contention by replying in the same manner. That is not why you are here. Don't let the conversation degrade. It may be time to say, "Look, I really want to talk about this but without us getting into a disagreement or making personal insults." "I didn't come here to insult you or fight. I understand if you are upset, but let's just talk this out." "I would appreciate it if you tell me how you feel without calling me names/insulting me or yelling." "I simply want to learn why you responded the way you did, and tell you how what you did made me feel."

Managing your emotions is vital during a confrontation. Confrontation doesn't have to mean contention.

Finally, if they are just unable to talk, then you can say, "I want you to know that I value you and the relationship we have. I want things to be better between us. That can't happen if we don't talk about it. If now is not a good time, or you need some time to prepare, that's fine too."

Whatever happens, try to *keep your cool.* Strength is revealed in the ability to restrain yourself. Managing your emotions is important during a confrontation. *Confrontation doesn't have to mean contention.*

Time outs. There are times when the other person you are dealing with may introduce a red herring, change the topic dramatically, insult you, or even have a breakdown. Or maybe you feel like you are at your limit emotionally. You need to know when to call a time out. When you feel caught off guard, that is the time to say - "Hold on, time out. Lets backtrack to why we are here having this discussion." It may help to even make the "T" symbol. This is a powerful nonverbal cue that can allow you to speak when someone is on a rant or everyone is just talking at once. Follow that with:

"Let's pause for a second."
"We need to not let our emotions carry us away."
"This is about (insert your issue), and not XYZ."

WHAT IS THE SCRIPT?

As you think about what you will say and how you will say it, try to settle on the best overall language to use. While speaking off of a piece of paper may not be what you are looking for, what you are looking for is to have a clearly thought out message. While the type of conversation, gravity, and timing will certainly need to be considered, here is a list of the the most common essential elements.

- Say something nice.
- Explain that you have something specific to talk about and although you want to hear from them, ask them to listen until you finish.
- Tell them why you are having this conversation and why this relationship matters.
- Tell them what you think happened. Let's review how we got here.
- Get their side of the story - what happened in their mind?
- Ask how they felt.
- Tell them how it made you feel.
- Tell them what you wish had happened.
- Ask if this makes sense and explain further if needed.
- Confirm what their intention was.
- Apologize if something you did may have influenced their negative behavior to you.
- Forgive them when they apologize.
- Commit to do better and ask them to try to do the same.
- Agree on what has been discussed.
- Always thank them for listening and sharing their feelings.

The Essentials

A few choice words. When we start with something nice, we highlight the good in others and honor the things that are admirable in their life. Combining this with statements explaining how you are feeling and why brings balance.

Exposing your feelings calmly in an honest and genuine way makes you vulnerable. Making yourself vulnerable will take the other person off of the offensive and prevent them from becoming defensive. Statements that allow you to be politely transparent encourage trust. Something like, "Let me be honest with you," is a good way to start. "I appreciate the way you x,y,z, and you have a lot of really great qualities like x,y,z." or, "I need to talk to you about x, because (it's bothering me/seems like it's bothering you/so and so)."

Write down 3 things you admire about the person. To be genuine you must believe the nice things you say. Make sure you identify and say things that you honestly believe, or at least can see the potential for.[10]

This exercise is also a way to shift your focus to the fact that they have potential and good in them. It will also motivate you to act without malice. As you spend some time being mindful and clear about the value of the other people in your life, you will be able to treat them as you would like to be treated. This simple exercise will help to prepare you mentally, physiologically and psychologically. You'll never be rude to anyone you respect.

At the end of the day we want to be hard on the issues but soft on the person – affirm your commitment to the relationship, and acknowledge what is going right in the relationship, as well as your view that a need exists to address the particular problem.

Apologies and forgiveness. Always be prepared to give an apology. Even if it is only for your delay in speaking up or otherwise. Apologies are a powerful tool for gaining trust and openness. A willingness to be imperfect on your part, not only shows humility, it also helps to disarm any defensiveness on the part of the other party.

The Heart of the Matter. Trying to get to the main issue is more important than hashing out details. *What are we talking about specifically?* Find the heart of the issue and write it down in a single statement if possible. "When you said, 'this thing' it made me feel like x." "I took that as if you were saying..." The more concise you can be in how you state this, the easier it is for others to understand you.

Getting to the Heart of the Matter

How it made you feel. This is often the most important part of *the heart of the matter.* How you felt and how the other people feel about the situation. These feelings often stem from a belief that is established by the previous actions (or the issue at hand), or which confirm a belief already held. These beliefs are things like: *Jane just doesn't like me, and that is why she is always upset with me.* Or, *I always get the lame jobs because Joe is the favorite.*

What you wish happened. How to go forward in a better way? What will we both try to do from now on?

Protocol will take you further than genius!

We have already outlined the most common essential elements in the most likely order. However, remember to respect time and place and use some wisdom. This means not barging in on others. It also means using your manners in greeting the person and making sure that they are not in the middle of something critical or time sensitive. Ask them if they have a few minutes, and be realistic about how much time you need. Be aware of onlookers. It is not polite to talk about sensitive information in front of others and you do not want to embarrass anyone. No one wants to be caught off guard, blindsided in a meeting, or exposed in front of others.

Try to have the conversation in a neutral place if available. Don't invite others to gang up on people, don't bring someone to a place they are uncomfortable and don't walk into their territory if they are upset with you already.

ENDING THE DISCUSSION

Bringing Closure

The end of a confrontation is hopefully better than the beginning. It is important to finish well. Any conversation that has weight to it, or some semblance of significance deserves to approached with caution and handled with care. Think of how a wound needs to be cleaned and dressed. Sometimes we have been wounded or hurt emotionally by the actions of others. A wound needs to be cleaned thoroughly, and then dressed properly. The part of cleaning involves opening, examining, and killing bacteria with antiseptic, as well as removing visible debris. It can be uncomfortable, painful even. However, if not done disease can set in, infection can spread, and death can even be a result. If one goes through the difficult process of this cleaning and does not bind, or close up the wound with a dressing, it can become dirty or open up again and the cleaning will have been for naught.

When we talk about confrontation, we are often looking at opening up a sensitive topic, examining, cleaning and treating it, and then closing it up. Bringing closure to any confrontation is this final step that will protect the hard work we have done to prepare and have the conversation in the first place. It will maintain the course of healing in the relationship as well.

Ask yourself, "Have we completed what we set out to do in the first place with this conversation? Did we correct what was out of order, clear up misunderstandings, and reconcile where there was strife?" If you need to apologize for your behavior or you got too heated, now is the time to let others know and apologize. If you have to even think twice about this or don't feel right about what you have said or how you said it, then it is better to apologize and be on the safe side.

Ending with a second recap and agreement. A solid recap or conclusion statement will do. Any assigned responsibilities, takeaways, and commitments must be *reiterated and owned by the appropriate parties*. To assume that there is total agreement and understanding is never wise. You must make sure. *It is often not enough for you to state the actions you expect of someone after the discussion; you must ask them to verbalize what they will do, or say yes.* Depending on the type of action, a timeline should be tied to it and affirmed as well. The same is true for any actions that are being asked of you. *Please, make sure that everyone has the same understanding by taking a moment to verbalize it.* Again, when it comes to concluding what took place and the result of the conversation, it is not enough for you to state what happened, and the outcome; others must be able to show their agreement and understanding by verbalizing it:

"You said that you felt insulted by my comments/actions, and I have apologized that you got that impression as it was not intended. Going forward, you will speak up if there is a problem, and I will strive to be more sensitive with how I communicate things to you."

Eye contact and even shaking on it make it genuine and allow you to detect any remorse or resistance. Depending on the situation and type of relationship, other physical affirmation may be appropriate, such as a hug, pat on the back, or shoulder/arm grab. In any business, professional or important situation, you should follow up with an email delineating what was discussed, agreed, and assigned as well as follow up if necessary. If you have a task or project management tool at work, that also can be appropriate.

After. What Next?

Emotional catch up. You and anyone else may need time to process what has happened. It has been commonly said that the heart is often a few steps behind the mind. Also, the best way to move past bad experiences (once dealt with), is with a positive experience. Find a way to do something positive as your next interaction with the person. This could be a meal, a game, or some other activity, as long as it is positive.

CHAPTER CONCLUSION

I hope that these tips will give you some practical steps to engage with others. Remember, strategies like this should be just one part of becoming a proficient communicator. We can all improve our overall ability to speak up, become more aware, and work on our perceptions. In so doing, we can become well rounded and effective in our relationships at home, with friends, and on the job.

CHAPTER 6

SIMPLE STRATEGIES FOR EFFECTIVE CONFRONTATION

"An eye for an eye leaves all the world blind"

In Chapter 3, we took an initial look at behaviors, what feeds those behaviors, and touched upon how to deal with them. Here we look at more strategies for dealing with those same characters as well as general tips for an effective verbal confrontation.

In my research for this book, I have discovered numerous online and radio outlets laden with recommendations to the general public from both bloggers and professional psychologists alike. Countless individuals daily seek advice from any place that they can find it. Most of these people are facing problems that they don't know how to handle. While this is no surprise, what is shocking is some of the advice given. This advice often encourages extreme responses to the imperfect behavior of others. Justifying a dysfunctional reaction to bad behavior is equally as wrong as the bad behavior itself. You may have heard that two wrongs don't make a right? The idea of harming those who wronged you is not new. Returning name calling for name calling doesn't solve the problems created by others calling you names. You may have heard it said that "an eye for an eye leaves the world blind." Perhaps this is true in a way. We have tragically become a society that tolerates the most base behavior because we also exhibit (at times) that same behavior. ***Change has to start somewhere.*** The answer is not to be as dysfunctional as everyone else. The answer is to learn how to deal with others without sinking to immaturity and emotional extremes. Learning to correct dysfunctional behavior in ourselves and address it with others is more straightforward than we may think. My goal for this chapter is to outline some simple steps that you can take. Hopefully, these ideas will help you prevent conversations from going south, and turn them around when it appears to be heading in that direction.

As we head into this topic, however, let me give you an example of some of the advice that I have seen out there. In one case, a woman and her husband had been happily married for several years. However, as they began to have some disagreements, they had trouble sorting things out and were avoiding each other. The husband would withdraw and his wife became increasingly more frustrated. Now there are many places to seek advice and some great sources out there on the internet. I have seen several professional counselors with successful blogs now advising people that when they encounter relational (marital) difficulties that it's probably just time to move on without trying to get help or even confront one another. Without a doubt, some circumstances would dictate moving on, or separation from the antagonizing parties until they can get help or change. However, if you married the love of your life and experienced excellent (or even decent) communication for years on end, then deciding to divorce over a new lack of communication is no small move. Unfortunately, this is the kind of advice from professionals out there. It is no wonder we have a society that is in trouble emotionally, physically, spiritually, financially, and relationally. *If there is a change in communication between you and your mate, there must be a reason or a cause.* Dealing with the source of contention is the only way to correct the situation. Running away will not deal with that cause. Those causes are often personal issues that arise from some experience or event. Sometimes they can be solved and resolved if addressed. That in itself involves a confrontation. *Moving on won't change you or the other person. Changing mates, jobs or location without addressing the underlying personal issues is just going to end up as moving from one mess to the next.* The baggage that created the problem with one mate will result in the same effects with a new mate. The behaviors and beliefs that caused you to have issues with your last two bosses or coworkers will likely persist with your next boss and coworkers. To stop the problems, the "messes," you must deal with the internal issues. **When it comes to relationships: it is the inner mess that creates the external.**

EXAMINE YOURSELF FIRST

Assuming we all looked at the cast of characters previously, I want you to ask yourself: What is my confrontation footprint? What is the result of my interactions with others? Is it a positive footprint or a negative? What do others walk away thinking and remembering about exchanges with me?

All of the behaviors mentioned in our cast qualified as defense mechanisms. Defenses are activated when you perceive that your security is threatened. Perhaps one of the most simple concepts is to demonstrate that you have the interest of others in mind. To do that effectively you will need actually to have it in mind. You will need to be clear about your motives and the why behind your approach.

Ask yourself: "What are my motives? Do I have the other person's interest in mind and if yes, how so?"

Let's move on to more simple strategies.

CREATE AN ENVIRONMENT WHERE IT'S SAFE TO SPEAK UP

If people feel stifled, or like they are walking on eggshells, this is not a safe environment. Regular and healthy dialogue is key to a safe speaking environment.[1] At work, this means time away from the desk is okay. At home this means turning off the television, having a meal together, and doing it often. Learn to foster an environment that includes regular conversation and welcomes truthfulness, opinions, and even some degree of respectful dissent or critiques. Let others know that it's safe for them to raise concerns and issues with you out in the open without fear of an adverse reaction.

Encourage individual input, and solicit feedback, by asking questions. For example: How am I doing? Are you okay with this? How does this approach make you feel? Do you understand why I am saying/said this? Does it make sense why we are doing it this way?[2]

Present issues by focusing on the facts and what concerns you about them. Describe what the person has done (door slamming, huffs and puffs, silent treatment) and give them an opportunity to explain why. Tell them what you expect and why.

Use "we." Although it's important to address people directly, use "I," "we" and "our," as opposed to "you" statements. Using "you" can put people on the defensive when the context is critical feedback. When using first-person pronouns, you convey how the behavior has impacted you and others and take the focus off of them by putting it on the actions, words spoken, and the outcomes. We could potentially lose this project if we don't keep our commitment to be at all weekly meetings.

In person. Confront passive-aggressive behavior in person to make sure your communication is understood, as opposed to using indirect means like email.

DEVELOP HEALTHY PATTERNS

The "issue" is not the issue; the pattern of behavior is the issue. Perhaps you can recognize some of these types of thinking and behavior? These deadly three must be identified and replaced.

Continuum-based thought vs. All-or-nothing thinking. All-or-nothing thinking is more than just my way or the highway; it is extremism of all types. This kind of thinking draws dramatic conclusions about events or people often based off of a singular example or instance and out of context. A lousy presentation is assumed to mean that you can't present. Successes make you think you are great, and a failure means you are trash. These conclusions are wrong because one win doesn't make a person outstanding, nor does a single failure determine that someone is a loser. Success and failure happen to all of us at various points in life. Replace this thinking with continuum-based and situation-based thinking. Examples could include, "I had a setback, but overall I am progressing," or "In this situation, I did well because I prepared." or, "I realize I need a different strategy (e.g. more preparation)."

Managed vs. Unmanaged emotions. We talked about overreacting, or when a person's behavior and emotions are way out of proportion to the circumstances. Those who fall prey to this pattern are often unable to control their own emotions (and may or may not regret them afterward). Managing emotions is worthy of a whole book. In short, addressing your feelings by thinking them through, and questioning whether they are justified is something we must all do. Learning to deal with emotions when by ourselves is a good step towards managing them when with others. In fact, one of the number one tips for not overreacting is not to react immediately. You heard that right. Let the moment pass to give yourself time to reason. When discussing how episodes of unchecked rage affect individuals, psychiatrist Dr. Diego Coira says that some people will realize the consequences of their actions and this will cause them to learn to change.[3] When taking time to think, challenge negative thoughts by examining the facts that dispel them.

Owning it vs. Blaming others. Blaming is a popular one to say the least. Learn to take responsibility for your actions and your inactions as well. Look for the ways you can improve and learn. Own your behavior, and you will be respected.

Once you start talking about these behaviors with others around you, it will become easier to call them out when they appear. Having shared goals with peers and friends to eliminate undesirable behaviors and develop healthy patterns will make it easier to recognize and make progress.

LEARN TO STAY CALM

Don't be emotional or get all worked up when confronted by others or upset about their actions. Speak to them in an even tone without raising your voice. Keep your hands down by your sides and try sitting down while you remain composed. When you are face-to-face with one of our characters, you will need to specify what you expect after you have gained their trust. Gaining trust means putting them at ease with your approach. Learning to balance an empathic approach with a firm conclusion by establishing boundaries or disciplinary action will help you to both understand, and expect different from them. A definite conclusion must be reached for the conversation to have a "success" outcome.

IDENTIFY THE CAUSE

Attempting to identify the cause of the behavior may take some patience as characters like PA's will need to be coaxed into telling you how they feel. You may need to call it out by stating, "It seems like you are not performing at your best lately. Did I do something to upset you?" Or "It seems like something is off, and I want to ask if it is a result of something I have done?" It may take several phases of gentle question asking to get to the bottom. Remember, these individuals are most likely to resist speaking up in the first place.

We must learn how to express ourselves appropriately. Setting and reinforcing boundaries, learning to listen as well as speak, affirming others (this does not signify that we agree with their views or what they have said), and practicing the art of diplomatic communication are all part of having healthy relationships.

We can influence what other people think, say or do to some degree. However, this is vastly limited to the level of control we can have over ourselves, specifically how we behave. It might be time to have a heart to heart and air how you feel with the people in your life - but it is always time to do it as a mature, self-controlled adult.

Ear statements or several statements that make use of the EAR components can help you engage or deal with an irate coworker and start a conversation with someone who is possibly upset or overreacting.[4]

E.A.R. STATEMENTS

Mediator and teacher Bill Eddy coined the term EAR Statement. I like this simple terminology for several reasons. The EAR acronym sounds just like ear, the part of the body with which you hear. The symbology of the ear reminds us that we need to assume a posture of listening, giving the other party attention and the opportunity to express themselves without fear or feeling threatened. They may still act threatened, but when we take the correct posture, we minimize those feelings. E.A.R. is an acronym for Empathy, Attention, and Respect. Bill teaches how to use these statements to deal with those who are in distress. The truth is, whether or not someone is upset, this method is excellent. Where high conflict personalities are concerned, it is crucial to remember that solid communication skills work best when coupled with kindness, patience, and compassion. These statements help you demonstrate that you are respectfully listening.

E. The Importance of Empathy

Empathy means being able to understand and share the feelings of another.

Merriam Webster defines empathy as the action of understanding. As in being aware of, being sensitive to, and vicariously experiencing the feelings, thoughts, and experience of another. Highly empathetic persons can do this without having the feelings and experience communicated in an objectively explicit manner. You get their gist.

Showing empathy for another person communicates that you care about what they are feeling and can relate to the feelings they are experiencing.

A. The Importance of Attention

"Being present" is commonly used today to differentiate between when others are not focused on what is happening around (or in front of) them versus being fully aware of the person, discussion, or task at hand. A person can be in the room, in a conversation, and yet be wandering in their thoughts. Showing that you are fully attentive also sends signals to the person with whom you are communicating. The greater your focus towards another, the more valued they will feel. There are many ways to let a person know that you will pay or are paying attention. For example, you can say, "I'm listening." You can look at the person, and sit down in front of them. You can be still without fidgeting or looking around. All of these actions serve to show that you are giving them attention. An EAR statement explicitly includes some verbal expression of your readiness to hear and that you are paying attention.

R. The Importance of Respect

Everyone has a fundamental need for respect from others. Every person deserves a basic level of respect as a fellow human being. Besides this, nearly everyone has something about them that you can respect, even if they are acting erratically. When we verbally communicate our respect for someone, it often has a placating effect.

Here are several statements showing respect:

"I recognize how much this matters to you." "Your faithfulness to see this through really impressed me." "I respect your punctuality and diligence." "I value (insert attribute), and you have shown you are that kind of a person." "We need the skills and experience you have."

When respect is genuine, we appear relatable, attentive, and affirm the person's value as an individual. An EAR statement can be broken up or can be one sentence such as, "I understand that you may feel frustrated or upset. I want you to know that I appreciate your opinion and value your patience in working this out." What matters is that it is sincere.

If the person still needs to vent, let them do so in as concise a manner as possible. Give them a few minutes, but don't be afraid to put a time stamp on the conversation. One more example is: "This is an important conversation, and I want to give it the attention it deserves. However, I have to be faithful to some other commitments. If you had to put how you feel and what you would like to happen in a few words, what would those words be?"

SETTING THE STAGE FOR THE FUTURE: BOUNDARIES WITH CONSEQUENCES

The most important thing (when faced with repeated bad actors) is to not only resolve the current crisis of communication but to try and set up new patterns of interaction. To do this, you need to be clear about what you are expecting from them going forward. Outline what you would each like to do differently, independent of the other. That is, even if they fail on their part, you will attempt to uphold yours and vice versa. Your piece could be checking in with them more proactively. Their part might be voluntarily participating and speaking up instead of hiding how they feel. You must (at a minimum) verbally confirm your expectations and agreement with them as often as necessary. It's also vital to set boundaries. If expectations are not met, there should be consequences.

In a work or professional setting, it becomes vital to confirm any agreements that you have. Put down assigned responsibilities and tasks (with due dates) in writing. Many people use project management tools or send summary emails at the close of a meeting. Drafting a quarterly plan or performance agreement is also a good idea. These tools only work, however, if you review progress and have regular accountability checkpoints.

When people feel that their insights and opinions are respected and welcomed, they are more likely to talk about issues.[5] Talking about matters helps to resolve them and prevent frustration or unwanted behaviors. It's okay to have problems, but it's not okay to do nothing about them.

EMOTIONAL AWARENESS

Focusing on Awareness

Maybe you have seen the pain scale at the hospital? It is that funny chart of facial expressions. Each facial expression reveals how a person is (likely) feeling when making that face. The same way a doctor or nurse can tell a person's pain or comfort level by their face, we need to be able to read the outward signs of others.

In a challenging conversation, you are looking to see how comfortable (or uncomfortable) the person you are confronting is.

Comfort cues signifying that a person is comfortable can include smiling, or neutral facial behavior, sitting, leaning, eye contact, and signs of listening. What about their breathing? Is it rapid, loud, and huffy? A neutral or relaxed posture with relaxed shoulders is also a better indication of comfort than a slouch or a tense stance. Do they have a natural cadence of speech with a neutral tone and normal volume? Some of these behaviors may vary by the individual, so use what you know to the best of your judgment.

Discomfort cues would include the opposite. Menacing postures, grimacing, angry, distressed, or upset facial expressions. Are they turning red? Shaking? Lurching or slouching, barely talking or shouting? Any extreme is a good indication that things are not going that well and they are uncomfortable.

In addition to the other person, of course, there is self-awareness; cognizance of our behavior.

Know your limits. Know when to say no. We must be self-aware and when necessary, recuse or excuse ourselves. Don't let emotions run your life, but let your life be your choice and take control of your feelings.

Running the engine too hot will lead to burn out or blow up! People will be hurt or let down if this happens.

Be persuasive by being genuine. You can soften your approach by lowering your voice, sitting down, and relaxing your arms. Think as you speak, choosing your words carefully. Speak slowly. Pay attention to the other person's expression. Don't run off on a rant or some long monologue.

Your reputation precedes you. It's true that those who know you also have an impression of your style. If you tend to be overly excited or loud, you will need to learn to restrain yourself. If you have the reputation of being quiet, it may take others a while to get used to a change in your behavior. One thing is for sure, having a positive reputation will make confrontation easier. People will not be afraid to talk to you if you can keep your cool. A person that never allows their emotions to cause them to mistreat others will be respected. The one who has control over their own emotions is the master of the situation.

Be Gracious. How you treat people matters. Credibility means having credit and is synonymous with being believable. You can draw from an established bank of what is known about you - your reputation, past experiences with you that may offset or cast a particular light on how others view your behavior. Having a good reputation means that when you blow it and own it, it is easy for others to see that your bad behavior is uncharacteristic of you. No one is infallible, and you will blow it sometimes. Everyone makes mistakes, including you and me. It is for this very reason that we should strive to be gracious when others overreact or do something questionable. We need to learn to give people the benefit of the doubt. Try questioning why you should think that they intentionally did something maliciously.

Non-verbal Ways to Show Respect.

Attentiveness

When it comes to conversations, you must both pay attention and demonstrate that you are paying attention. Think about what your facial expression is saying. Are you looking at the person, leaning forward or actively listening? Remember: No fidgeting, looking at your phone or the clock. Don't take any calls if at all possible. If there is an emergency, explain yourself. If you have a time limit, be clear about it up front.

Here are some basic tips:

Don't roll your eyes, make noises of discomfort, or interrupt. No name calling, sarcasm or insults. If you can't handle the conversation or just aren't prepared, be honest and say, "Time out. I need a minute to process here. Can we reconvene when I have had time to think?" If you are taxed, stressed, or overtired, then say so and ask respectfully to be excused. Some people can't help but try to push your buttons. A word to the wise: don't take the bait. Taking the bait means giving in to emotional responses instead of keeping your cool.

Pause as you speak with others and try to think - is this what I want to happen here? Am I taking the bait or working towards my goal? You can say no to frustration and keep control of yourself by reminding yourself of your goals, who you are and who you want to be. If you see that you are getting frustrated in any way, remember it will be well worth the effort to hold your tongue or walk away.

In the midst of conversations, you must know why am I are here and what is it I want out of this conversation? Is it reasonable, right, and mutually beneficial? Is my method straightforward, honest, and honorable? Would I want to be dealt with in this same manner? Is my attitude appropriate, kind, and considerate? Am I respectful, truthful and to the point?

Watch people's level of engagement - withdrawing or advancing will reveal their comfort level. Both a hard withdraw and a hard advance reveal discomfort. Casual or energetic dialogue with respect and comfort clues are the goal.

Withdrawing can include intentionally ambiguous communication. What is it they are not saying or not saying directly?

At this point, you might be feeling that overwhelmed. What if these strategies don't seem to work, or I fail at using them? The answer is; at some point, you and the tips most likely will fail, and guess what, it's okay. The formula is not perfect. The goal is not to be perfect. The goal is to improve and strive to do what is right.

Getting Back to Why

Intentional change is going to take some focus. You will need to have an anchor to keep you motivated when it seems harder than you thought. Your "why" is this anchor. *Why* am I working to change even though it's currently uncomfortable, inconvenient, and somewhat scary? Does this relationship matter? Does my reputation and how I treat people matter? It is the answers to these questions that can help you to stay motivated and focused on long-term growth. While some people will rationalize and justify their failures, a mature person admits mistakes, apologizes, and seeks to grow.

When things don't work out, don't take the bait to get upset, angry or distracted! Be focused. Embrace the journey to the destination. You will have some mistakes and not always be successful in getting to the conclusion you want with others.

Communication is the Currency of Life

Relationships are all about communication. Communication is where we exchange with one another. We can gain or lose by trading thoughts, ideas, and emotional energy. We also feel valued (or not) by how others react to our words.

Energy can be contagious. The spirit of another person can bring you up or bring you down. What kind of mood are you bringing with you to work, meetings, intimate relationships, and your daily cadence of interactions?

We must be successful in communicating to be successful in life. Most problems in life are just communication problems. Most of the time a miscommunication is just a lack of clear (or any) communication. We somehow miss in the communication process.

One reason many people today are overwhelmed at work and on their job is due to a lack of communication. We must learn when to speak up, and when to say no. For managers, this also means listening by asking questions. The number one reason people are in disagreements is the inability to communicate effectively. That means having a dialogue and not "talking at" someone.

We need to learn how to communicate and plan for effective communication by recognizing how we derail ourselves and others from sharing their position.

SOW TO REAP

Often we want to see immediate results in everything that we do, and while it is certainly possible to get immediate improvements, it may take time for people to recognize how we have changed. Just because we plant the seeds doesn't mean we will see an immediate crop. It may not come as a surprise that you must put something in to get something out. We must care for the people in our ecosystem. We should never expect a harvest of something that we haven't sown.

Seed your ecosystem by being friendly, encouraging, kind, and honest. Build trust so that when you need it, it's there. The best way you can to do this is to keep your word. We must establish patterns of keeping our word. One way for us to do this is to stop oversubscribing or committing to so many things that we can't possibly deliver on them all.

In the end, regardless of your current reputation, it is possible to position yourself as someone who cares. We can all learn how to diffuse a difficult situation, even when we are caught off guard. Being your best at all times will mean improving your basic patterns of communication and pausing enough (before you speak) to make sure you don't take the bait or revert to old habits. Use EAR statements to calm people who are upset and move forward. Pay attention to others and yourself. Watch for verbal and nonverbal signals. By doing all of these things, you can master the simple strategies and improve your confrontation and communication skills overall.

CHAPTER CHECKLIST

Don't subscribe to everything you hear. Relationships can be improved and are worth the work.

Know yourself; assess your motives, attitude, and intent towards others.

Show an interest in the opinions of others and make them feel comfortable by not interrupting, dismissing, or disparaging them.

Don't fall for passing blame, all or nothing thinking, or emotional extremes.

Use Ear Statements to gain trust, calm others, and signal that you are listening.

When attacked or confronted by bad behavior, don't take the bait to retaliate.

Set clear boundaries with bad actors - make sure they understand where they crossed the line.

Grow in awareness by observing yourself and others.

Remind yourself why it matters (e.g. your personal growth) in order to keep yourself motivated.

————————————————

7

CONTINUAL SELF-TRANSFORMATION

What Can I Do to Keep Improving?

Understand the Journey
Embrace Discomfort
Find Your Voice
Believe in Yourself
Do it for Others

As we close this book out, I want to leave you with ways that you can stick to the process and keep growing as a person. Ways that you can apply the DWIP (dee-whip).

HOW TO APPLY THE DEAL WITH IT PHILOSOPHY?

By now you should have seen numerous ways to tackle problems and understand that executing the strategies and techniques are the path to using the philosophy. Pay the

163

parking ticket. Ask the questions. Take out the trash. Sign up for the class. Follow through on doing what you know you should as soon as it is reasonably sensible.

UNDERSTAND THE JOURNEY

It's not what you get by reaching your destination that matters most — it's what you become in the process.

The athlete who decides that he or she is in shape and can take a year off will soon discover that the saying, "use it or lose it," is true. Capabilities in life can be increased by exercise and use, whether physical fitness, mental sharpness or soft skills. To be our best, we must be committed to a lifestyle of development. This book, classes, and lessons learned are not just events but forces that propel us on our journey. Embrace the journey.

By use, you gain, and by disuse, you lose. By application, you increase. You increase by doing, and you decrease by doing nothing. Therefore you must do and continue to do.

There are many reasons people fail to get lasting results with diets. One common reason is that they see a diet as a temporary sacrifice to achieve a goal.[1] However, those who want to maintain a state of health realize that keeping the diet is the key. If you are currently unhealthy or overweight, then you must change your lifestyle to be healthy. You don't need another diet - just an overhaul, ☺. A second misconception is that an "overhaul" requires an immediate and dramatic change in behavior.[2] The "all at once," radical shift rarely works for behavioral changes. Instead, it is step-by-step changes that lead to success. A gradual and consistent change with small modifications is easier to handle and maintain. For example, let's say first, you might cut out pastries or indulgences during the week. Second, you replace candy bar snacks with popcorn or trail mix. Third, you begin to check your portion sizes or balance meals across more food types by adding greens. The list goes on and on. The key here is that the change in behavior is progressive.

The dramatic and instant changes must be in our mindset. Once we are committed to specific action mentally and emotionally, then behavior changes will continue to follow. You must be resolute in your commitment to who you are going to be. Become that person intentionally, yet gradually. If you read through chapter 4, then you already understand that true personal transformation isn't necessarily a quick fix.

BELIEVE IN YOURSELF

Your metamorphosis involves you working to pull a better you out from the inside. Although many parts of an interpersonal makeover are pragmatic, the actual change is much more profound; it is finding your inner call (desire) and responding. It is you developing a clear image of yourself, accepting and loving yourself. It is becoming a person of action, of voice. It is the process of learning to speak and move out of growing confidence in who you are, what you are called to do, and how you can contribute. You must bring forth your contribution.

What you speak and how you express yourself will always be unique because you are unique. The goal of this book was not to give you a formula so you can robotically go through the motions. Instead, it is to convince you of the validity and benefit of getting hands-on with your life and society, to show you how to unravel hindrances and use the right tools to tackle situations that might make you uncomfortable.

So, while it is great to get inspiration from others and seek to emulate the positive traits and habits we observe, we can only ever succeed in being ourselves. It is your uniqueness that makes you indispensable. Therefore, the transformation is in knowing your skin and getting comfortable in it. You become authentic when you reveal your true self. That self will undoubtedly change over time but you can't simply hide yourself away and expect to feel fulfilled.

> *To become more successful, you do not have to change who you are--you have to become more of who you are... who you are at your best so you can create better relationships, grow your business, and become intensely valuable to those who matter most. - Sally Hogshead.*

You have to own it! You are beautiful! You are unique. Own it! Do you! Be Yourself! Give what you got! Say it with me right now: "I am beautiful, and I will give what I've got!"

Confidence is key to success in business, relationships, and life. Confidence or self-assurance can raise your intelligence. Fear freezes the brain, paralyzing ability. Whether on a test, on stage, in a meeting, before a stunt or sporting activity of any kind.

"There has been a very, very big lobby within educational psychology against the notion of IQ," notes psychologist Chamorro-Premuzic of Goldsmiths University in London. "And part of this lobby has been based on the idea that self-perceptions matter more than actual ability." Tomas Chamorro-Premuzic Confidence enables intelligence to work. Allow the intelligence you have to work at its best by believing in your abilities and potential to increase them.

EMBRACE DISCOMFORT

Problems and obstacles are part of life. Trusting that every potential problem also has a solution will help you to act, not necessarily without fear, but in spite of it. Knowing that most problems can be fixed (even if it doesn't work out the first time) is empowering, liberating, and hopefully motivating.

LEARN TO SPEAK UP

You must speak up. Remember: *Being vulnerable is being brave.* Be Brave.

How to Start: Build Confidence
with These Small Steps:

Smile More - Smiling builds confidence.

Look People in the Eye - You can practice by looking yourself
in the mirror. Remember the person is a human being just
like you! They have fears, failures and insecurities. They
want to be loved and appreciated. Perhaps the most bristly
among us are those who have already been so disappointed
and are the most afraid.

Join in Casual Conversations - Practice speaking up when
the stakes are lower! Get used to hearing your own voice
and participating.

Say Hello to People you Meet - Practice being bold and
friendly.

Attend a Networking Event - Talk with some strangers.

Practice Alone - Work on your conversation skills by saying
positive things about yourself and others, talking about your
goals, your life. Do it out loud.

Read Out Loud - Simply hearing your voice constantly
builds confidence.

Name Your Fears - Ask yourself, "Why am I afraid?"
Identifying and naming a fear reduces its power and helps
you put it in perspective.

Practice Honesty - Integrity is the source of a clean conscience and a clean conscience creates confidence and a sense of power. When you start with honesty, people are more likely to listen attentively.

Call Someone - You know someone you should call, just do it.

Apologize Quickly - It's okay to be wrong; it's not okay to pretend you are right.

HOW TO SAY "NO"

"The difference between successful people and very successful people is that very successful people say no to almost everything." - Warren Buffett

Learning to say *No* is vitally important. As a part of our development, we all need to realize that using the "N" word (No), is something that most of us need to make a habit. The great teacher, Jesus, once said, "Let your yes be yes, and your no be no." This saying means that whatever we say, we should stick to it and learn not only to be decisive but committed to our decisions. Here are some thoughts on how to grow in your use of the "polite no."

Just Do It

Just say it. It has to merely be spoken, emailed, or made clear professionally or politely.

No is a Complete Sentence

There is just no reason that you have to elaborate. "No is the answer." "My answer is no." No means no. There is nothing else to discuss. Offering explanations can be a trap, so avoid it and no matter what, don't lie. You must be genuine, and you can say something to the effect of: "For various (or personal) reason(s) at this time I need to decline (politely). I hope that you can respect my decision. My decline doesn't necessarily mean I don't want to," (although it may, and that is fine). It may be a permanent No, or it may be, "I may be willing to help next year, month, time, always feel free to ask." In any case, sticking with a simple No is always a good option.

Practice Makes Perfect

Practice regularly - in front of the mirror and if possible with a friend. Let the friend role play for you and ask you to do random things. Pay careful attention to how you feel, how you position yourself. Inhale deeply, sit up or stand up straight with your shoulders back, and look them straight in the eye and say, No. Practice saying it affirmatively. Listen to your voice - do not quaver, yet don't be upset. Picture yourself in a place of freedom and joy, and with firm yet warm confidence, say No.

Saying No is Good for You

Understand why saying No is good for you - review your priorities. Saying No allows you to focus on the most important things, or the priorities that matter now. Being focused makes you more effective in serving yourself and others.

Understanding Your Self-worth is a Key to Saying No

Understand why you might not want to say No - what are the roots? Are you afraid of rejection or losing your job? Does it make you feel valuable to be asked to do things? Are you scared that people won't ask anymore if you say no and you will be left out? Find out where these thoughts come from and realize that they are often fear-based and deceptive. You are valuable, period. Pulling yourself in a million directions will not make you productive. We all need to find where we fit best, so we can contribute at our best. You must give yourself a chance to improve by making time to work on yourself. You must take care of you to be able to help others effectively. If you are always saying "yes" because it makes you feel good to be wanted, then your motives are a clue to the fact that something needs to change. Don't use overcommitment to combat a fear of rejection, insecurity, or low importance. We should seek to serve not to cover our self-doubts, but to contribute genuinely. In our personal lives, this means to love and benefit our inner circle, our community, and society. At work, this means finding ways to contribute holistically and logically based on our job, role, position, and the goals of the company - without neglecting our core responsibilities and duty. It also means not burning yourself out or overworking, which drives the quality of your contribution down. Don't seek to prove your worth, but look for ways to add benefit because you have value to add.

It's also okay to offer an alternative if you have one in mind. Whether that be suggesting another person for them to ask, another day or time to participate, or another activity altogether is up to you. As long as its genuine and you are sure of your offer.

DITCH PROCRASTINATION

The antidote for procrastination is *action*. The cure for fear is *action*. The best way to stop feeling down is *action*. Massive action can lead to massive results, but it's not always necessary to take massive action, just some action. You must do it now, immediately, *today*. Initial action is the key. You must do *something* to start, and taking a second action equals progress. The third action is momentum. If you have ever seen the videos of people toppling dominoes that are consecutively larger and larger, the same principle of inertia is at work in a different fashion. The best way to quit stalling is make a list of things you can do right now and do at least one of them. Commit to doing something to change every day and then schedule it on your calendar, put a reminder on your phone, tell someone about it and be accountable to them. Write your one action in the margin of this book. Bravery is not fearlessness but action in the face of fear.

FAILURE IS A LEARNING EXPERIENCE

Sometimes we experience what we perceive as failure in our initial actions, but that failure is only temporary if we keep moving and refining our strategy. Learning is part of the process and that means multiple attempts may be required for the results we want. By acting and trying, you will learn what works and what doesn't. So then confidence is not arrogance or pride, but a sense of being growable, teachable, and able to improve. Self-assurance is moving with purpose, humbly knowing that you must do something for things to happen. Change requires doing. Confidence makes your ambitions and goals reachable. It won't necessarily get them served to you on a platter, but it will make them attainable by reducing the impact of fears. Remember that the point is not to feel comfortable but to do what you know to be "best" despite the discomfort. Why? Because doing what is right is success and any agitation is typically temporary. Confidence isn't believing that you know how to do everything, but rather the belief that you can learn to do things, and commitment to see through what you set out to do to the end. If you need to ask for help, confidence allows you to do that without fear of feeling or looking inferior. It takes courage to admit what you don't know rather than to pretend you know. Attempting to cover up deficiency is pride combined with insecurity. Confidence and humility go hand in hand.

Success = Doing What We Know to be Right

KEEP REFINING. REFLECTION, FEEDBACK, AND EXPERIMENTING

Just as challenging and uncomfortable as it might seem to speak your mind or call out others, it can also be painful to hear from others. It is necessary that we learn to embrace feedback.

Feedback is helpful information that is given to someone so they know what they can do to improve.

Remember the cues we discussed? Facial expressions, posture, the tone of voice, word choice, and many other factors are feedback. Feedback in that sense can merely be the response or returned reaction from an action or input. A person's response (whether subtle or extreme) reveals their comfort level. Their response clues us in on how well we are communicating.

We have learned that recognizing this kind of feedback is part of social awareness and a crucial factor in analyzing and increasing one's EQ, or emotional quotient.[4]

Feedback goes far beyond these simple Conversational Condition Clues™. What we are discussing now is typically a conversation after "the conversation." Feedback in this sense is something or someone that can help us answer the question, "How am I doing at this?" If you have determined that you need to improve your communication skills, you may have done it based on both your perception (self-advised feedback) and the reactions of others.

Regardless of whether the author of this book knows you, the helpful tools, tips, and techniques in this book can both inform you and enable you to change your communication. While this book is useful, we also need on location, or in situation feedback from others, and indeed we know that it is an ultimately unstoppable or non-negotiable fact that we will receive some feedback. We can, therefore, make some decisions about how we receive feedback from others.

We can take control over the value that feedback brings to us by recognizing several things;

If we choose to embrace and seek feedback on our own (periodically or after a situation that was difficult, we alter the mix of information and quality of feedback we receive as well as the terms on which it is given - we are more in control of the feedback session and better prepared mentally and emotionally for the feedback provided.

We must understand that the person giving feedback is not perfect, that they have their opinion and viewpoint, and that their assumptions or conclusions may or may not be correct.

We must weigh what the person has said objectively and determine what, if anything, is valuable to us. We may conclude that a particular individual is not a good source of feedback, or we may accept some of what they have said for consideration.

We need to be secure in who we are regardless of what others think, but that doesn't mean that their thoughts are unimportant or incorrect. It may only be that something we are doing is triggering an adverse reaction in that person. This trigger may not be because what we have done is wrong or insensitive but because the person may have an emotional trauma or memory from the past that created a wound or false belief. The mistaken belief is a trigger point that is activated by situations similar or that can be associated with the circumstances when the belief was created.

Tips for Receiving Critical Feedback:

Be comfortable with who you are. You are the one who gets to define your identity and work on living out your values.

Separate their emotions from their information (focus on the information as primary).

Understand what values they have and how that may be affecting their perspective.

Validate the information shared as true or false with other inputs if necessary.

Use the information and feedback given to assess specific actions. Do not use the input to label yourself or to develop some immutable interpretation of who you are.

Determine how you will use the information given to adjust your actions and live in a way that is consistent with your values.

Here are Some More Tips for Soliciting
Feedback That is Situation (Event) Specific:

It should be close enough to the event that it can be remembered easily.
After the event has cooled off (if it was intense) - emotions are lower, and evaluations change.
Be specific in soliciting input. What was your impression of my tone and manner when I said this…?
Do it in a safe space that is neutral and semi-private. Preferably face to face. A cafe, hotel lobby, or park.

Who should you ask? Not just anyone. You should have developed enough rapport to ask this person. Conversely, sometimes a long-time associate is so familiar with you that they may have a hard time being honest or recognizing what is a fault or an area for change. They may chalk up your behavior as part of "the way you are," and sometimes that is not helpful to personal transformation. They may also be uncomfortable with you making progress in life (especially if they are not making any).

Someone that has less to lose is likely to be honest and independent.

DO IT FOR OTHERS

Find your courage for others.

Speaking up and shutting up both have consequences. What kind? Well for one, telling people what you think might help you to get what you want or at least some of what you want. Getting what you want may be a necessity at work to get the job done. Getting what you want at home will make you happier and more pleasurable to be around. Provided that your "want" isn't illegal, or harmful to others and yourself, getting what you want isn't a bad thing.

The best way to get what you desire in life is to make what you want about others, and not yourself. Then everyone benefits. Think about the Good Samaritan. He got what he wanted in helping the man who had been robbed, and indeed, the man helped got something he desperately needed and wanted. The Good Samaritan used his money or his resources to help others. *In our case, we are discussing the use of our words. When we recognize the weight and impact of our words and how they can be a benefit to others, we begin to use more discretion.* The consequences of not speaking up, or refusing to listen, can be more harmful than the potential outcomes of a confrontation.

Hopefully, you now see that *Dealing with It* isn't about pointing the finger at others as much as it is about turning the finger at ourselves. We need to transform our thinking as a whole. That means confronting our perspectives, desires, and motives. It means taking time to reflect on who you are and who you would like to become. Ask yourself, what matters to me? How do I want to be known? What will my life have meant to others? In considering such questions, we get to the core of our behavior. There are always reasons why we do the things we do. One way to reduce conflicts and become more effective when facing them is to change our habits. Hopefully, as you have gone through this book until now, you are beginning to understand that dealing with issues is necessary, doesn't have to be painful, and can even be satisfying. Changing our identity is fundamental to making lasting changes in our behavior.[5] Right now each of us is sitting with our best friend and worst enemy - ourselves! Our thoughts and behavior are what set us up for success or failure. You can decide:

I want to be more assertive
I will be forthcoming and truthful
When I am upset, I will let others know why
When others upset me, I will let them know
If I can't do something, I will say no
If I need something, I will ask

Telling Yourself These Key Ideas Can Help You Succeed:

I know what I want
I am not afraid to speak up
Others generally are open to my opinion
When there are problems with others, I am confident that we can work them out
Taking care of issues right away prevents them from ballooning or becoming permanent
I can ask for help when I need it
I am okay with learning as I go
Progress today is better than hoping for perfection that never comes

These kinds of statements can become a part of a Personal Values Statement. A Personal Values Statement is a description of how you see yourself and what values matter to you. It is easier to live a better life once you have identified who you want to be and why. Defining what that life looks like will help you plan it and work on it. You can become healthy, confident, and compassionate. You can acquire the skills you need and improve over time. Eventually, you develop the ability to approach others, to help others. If you can't help yourself change, how can you expect or demand it of others?

We have now gone beyond dealing with problems, to the reasons that we should: satisfaction in a fulfilling, purposeful and meaningful life. By improving ourselves, we better our world, and by seeking to improve our society, we are forced to learn, to improve ourselves.

I want to leave you with this final thought. Learning takes humility, but it also takes guts. I want to commend you for being teachable, and brave. If you made it this far you have more courage than you realize. Keep moving forward! As you strive to apply the principles in this book, learning will become practice. It will get down into your heart and become a lifestyle of acting on your best intentions. It's as we keep the commitments we make to ourselves that we begin to make real progress in life. Be brave, overcome your fears, express your feelings, and change the world with me.

END NOTES

CITATIONS

Online References follow this format: Site, Author, Date Published (if available), Article Name. All links verified last as of September 2018

In Print Materials cited by Title, Author, Date.

Chapter 1

1. Psychologytoday.com, Hara Estroff Marano, August 23, 2003. Procrastination: Ten Things To Know, https://www. psychologytoday.com/us/articles/200308/procrastination-ten-things-know, 8.25.18
2. Katrina Brown Hunt, January 4, 2012, America's Rudest Cities,https://www.travelandleisure.com/slideshows/americas-rudest-cities, 8.25.18
3. https://www.bbc.com/news/technology-31749753, Why are people so mean to each other online? 26 March 2015, By Jane Wakefield
4. https://www.sciencedaily.com/releases/1999/10/991021094811. htm, Old Brains Can Learn New Tricks: Study Shows Older People Use Different Areas Of The Brain To Perform Same

'Thinking Task' As Young http://skillcookbook.com/aging/ How age helps learning

5.   https://www.scientificamerican.com/article/tough-choices-how-making/, https://www.nytimes.com/2011/08/21/magazine/do-you-suffer-from-decision-fatigue.html?pagewanted=all, https://www.entrepreneur.com/article/244395

6.   Leviticus, 19:17, Matthew 18:15

Chapter 2

1.   Psychology Today, Shoba Sreenivasan, Ph.D., and Linda E. Weinberger, Ph.D., December 14, 2016, Why We Need Each Other, https://www.psychologytoday.com/us/blog/emotional-nourishment/201612/why-we-need-each-other

2.   patheos.com, Rabbi Rami, March 6, 2014, 4 Two Jews, Three Opinions https://www.patheos.com/blogs/rabbiramishapiro/2014/03/4-two-jews-three-opinions/

3.   inc.com, Amy Morin, 7 Toxic Thinking Mistakes That Will Keep You From Being Mentally Strong, March 5, 2018 https://www.inc.com/amy-morin/7-thinking-patterns-that-will-that-rob-you-of-mental-strength-and-what-you-can-do-about-them.html; Psychology Today, Susan Krauss Whitbourne Ph.D., The Essential Guide to Defense Mechanisms, October 22, 2011. https://www.psychologytoday.com/us/blog/fulfillment-any-age/201110/the-essential-guide-defense-mechanisms

4.   takingcharge.csh.umn.edu, Karen Lawson, MD, How Do Thoughts and Emotions Affect Health?, https://www.takingcharge.csh.umn.edu/how-do-thoughts-and-emotions-affect-health

5.   medicaldaily.com, Samantha Olson, Knowledge Is Brain Power, Sept 10, 2014, http://www.medicaldaily.com/knowledge-brain-power-how-stop-shrinking-your-brain-and-improve-your-thought-process-302450

6.   drdufford.com, Donald Dufford, Ph.D., Anger Issues, https://www.drdufford.com/anger-issues/

7. Nature.com, REDD1 is essential for stress-induced synaptic loss and depressive behavior, Kristie T Ota, Rong-Jian Liu, Bhavya Voleti, Jaime G Maldonado-Aviles, Vanja Duric, Masaaki Iwata, Sophie Dutheil, Catharine Dum, Steve Boikess, David A Lewis, Craig A Stockmeier, Ralph J DiLeone, Christopher Rex, George K Aghajanian& Ronald S Duman, Published: 13 April 2014, http://www.nature.com/nm/journal/v20/n5/full/nm.3513.html

8. adrenalfatigue.org, Dr. James L. Wilson, Cortisol & Adrenal Function, https://adrenalfatigue.org/cortisol-adrenal-function/)

9. Yale News, Bill Hathaway, Yale team discovers how stress and depression can shrink the brain, August 12, 2012, http://news.yale.edu/2012/08/12/yale-team-discovers-how-stress-and-depression-can-shrink-brain

10. PsychCentral, Terry L. Ledford, Ph.D., Choosing Not to Get Upset, July 8, 2018, https://psychcentral.com/blog/choosing-not-to-get-upset/

11. PsychCentral, Margarita Tartakovsky, M.S., How Conflict Can Improve Your Relationship, https://psychcentral.com/lib/how-conflict-can-improve-your-relationship/; Law Offices of William M. Strachan, William Strachan, Conflict Can Be Good for Your Relationship, February 5, 2015, https://www.williamstrachanfamilylaw.com/2015/02/conflict-good-relationship/ ; Psychology Today, Elizabeth Dorrance Hall Ph.D., Why Conflict Is Healthy for Relationships, March 23, 2017, https://www.psychologytoday.com/us/blog/conscious-communication/201703/why-conflict-is-healthy-relationships

12. Developing the Qualities of Success, Zig Ziglar, 2015.

13. Matthew 7:12

14. Ed Cole Library, Ed Cole, Coleisms, http://www.edcole.org/index.php?fuseaction=coleisms.searchColeisms

15. Online Etymology Dictionary, peace, http://www.etymonline.com/index.php?term=peace

16. Psychology Today, Susan Krauss Whitbourne Ph.D., Why the Emotionally Intelligent May

Earn More Money, October 3, 2017, https://www.psychologytoday.com/us/blog/fulfillment-any-age/201710/why-the-emotionally-intelligent-may-earn-more-money

Chapter 3

1. Pshychologytoday.com, Adam Alter, May 17, 2010, Why It's Dangerous to Label People, https://www.psychologytoday.com/us/blog/alternative-truths/201005/why-its-dangerous-label-people

2. a.) ncbi.nlm.nih.gov, Marleen M. Rijkeboera, Gerly M. de Boob., Nov 10, 2009, Early maladaptive schemas in children, https://www.ncbi.nlm.nih.gov/pubmed/19944408, https://www.sciencedirect.com/science/article/pii/S0005791609000792, Faculty of Social Sciences, Department of Clinical and Health Psychology, Utrecht University, Utrecht, The Netherlands.

   b.) sciotests.com, Dr. Simon Moss, 7/21/2016Early maladaptive schemas, http://www.sicotests.com/psyarticle.asp?id=448

   c.) Self-Matters:Creating Your Life from the Inside Out, Phil McGraw, 2001 d.) Schematherapy.com, Early Maladaptive Schemas, Schema Therapy Institute, .http://www.schematherapy.com/id63.htm

3. Bandler, Richard & John Grinder (1976). Patterns of the Hypnotic Techniques of Milton H. Erickson, M.D. Volume 1. Cupertino, CA :Meta Publications. ISBN 0-916990-01-X, Erickson & Rossi - Hypnotic Realities

4. Tosey, P. & Mathison, J., (2006) "Introducing Neuro-Linguistic Programming." Centre for Management Learning & Development, School of Management, University of Surrey.

5. Bandura A. Self-efficacy: The exercise of control. New York: Freeman; 1997.

6. Crucial Conversations: Tools for Talking When Stakes Are High, Joseph Grenny, Al Switzler, Ron McMillan, 2002

7. See 2

8. Allaboutthewaltons.com,The Waltons, The Career Girl. http://www.allaboutthewaltons.com/ep-s5/s05-17.php

9. alberttellis.org, The Albert Ellis Institute, Haley Elder, M.A., http://alberttellis.org/poor-me-syndrome-pms/

10. alberttellis.org, The Albert Ellis Institute, Haley Elder, M.A., http://alberttellis.org/poor-me-syndrome-pms/

11. psychologytoday.com, Guy Winch Ph.D., 7 Ways to Get Out of Guilt Trips, May 16, 2103, https://www.psychologytoday.com/us/blog/the-squeaky-wheel/201305/7-ways-get-out-guilt-trips

12. phrases.org, The Attaché; or, Sam Slick in England, 1843/4, Thomas C. Haliburton, https://www.phrases.org.uk/meanings/fly-off-the-handle.html

13. drjuliehanks.com, Julie Hanks, How to Stop Overreacting, http://www.drjuliehanks.com/2011/02/02/how-to-stop-overreacting-keep-your-cool/

14. http://www.angermgmt.net, Leonard Ingram, http://www.angermgmt.net

15. mindtools.com, How to Manage Passive-Aggressive People, https://www.mindtools.com/pages/article/passive-aggressive-people.htm

16. psychologytoday.com, Rosemary K.M. Sword, Philip Zimbardo Ph.D., Oct 25, 2013. https://www.psychologytoday.com/blog/the-time-cure/201310/toxic-relationships-part-ii

17. stopbullying.gov, An official website of the United States government. https://www.stopbullying.gov

18. littlehouseontheprairie.com, Season 3, Episode 9, The Bully Boys, http://littlehouseontheprairie.com/little-house-on-the-prairie-episode-guide-season-3/

19. imbd.com, Back to the Future, https://www.imdb.com/title/tt0088763/

Chapter 4

1. Self-Matters: Creating Your Life from the Inside Out, Phil McGraw, 2001

2. a.) Self-Matters:Creating Your Life from the Inside Out, Phil McGraw, 2001.

    b.) Transactional Analysis in Psychotherapy, Eric Berne 1961, http://changingminds.org/explanations/models/life_scripts.htm

3. https://www.simplypsychology.org/self-concept.html; https://www.elsevier.com/connect/the-5-most-powerful-self-beliefs-that-ignite-human-behavior, Bobby Hoffman, PhD.

4. Dictionary.com

5. Martin Seligman, 1991

6. tripod.com, The Lost Deep Thoughts, http://jackhandey6.tripod.com/david/id14.html

7. Ziglar, Zig, Developing the Qualities of Success: How to Stay Motivated, 2010

8. psychcentral.com, Therese J. Borchard, psychcentral.com/blog/archives/2013/11/30/words-can-change-your-brain, huffingtonpost.com, James Clear, Sep 25, 2017, http://www.huffingtonpost.com/james-clear/positive-thinking_b_3512202.html

9. sciencedirect.com, Journal of Research in Personality, Volume 10, Issue 2, AbrahamTesser, June 1976, Attitude polarization as a function of thought and reality constraints, https://www.sciencedirect.com/science/article/pii/0092656676900714.

10. firstpeople.us, Two Wolves, A Cherokee Legend, http://www.firstpeople.us/FP-Html-Legends/TwoWolves-Cherokee.html

11. firstpeople.us, Two Wolves, A Cherokee Legend, http://www.firstpeople.us/FP-Html-Legends/TwoWolves-Cherokee.html

12. Ziglar, Zig, Developing the Qualities of Success: How to Stay Motivated, 2010,

13. ABC Science, abc.net.au, Kylie Andrews, August 7, 2013, The importance of kelp forests, http://www.abc.net.au/science/photos/2013/08/07/3816861.htm

14. Center for Substance Abuse Treatment (US). Trauma-Informed Care in Behavioral Health Services. Rockville (MD): Substance Abuse and Mental Health Services Administration (US); 2014. (Treatment Improvement Protocol (TIP) Series, No. 57.)

Chapter 3, Understanding the Impact of Trauma. Available from: https://www.ncbi.nlm.nih.gov/books/NBK207191/

15. psychologytoday.com, Linda Wasmer Andrews, Jul 14, 2017, How a Sense of Purpose in Life Improves Your Health.
Forbes.com, Alice G. Walton, Oct 7, 2010, The Science Of Giving Back: How Having A Purpose Is Good For Body And Brain

16. Forgive for Good, Fred Luskin, 2001

17. psychologytoday.com, Christopher Bergland, Apr 11, 2015, Holding a Grudge Produces Cortisol and Diminishes Oxytocin. Dryburgh, N. (2014). Oxytocin as a Moderator of Attachment Orientation and Forgiveness. *Western Undergraduate Psychology Journal*, 2 (1). Retrieved from https://ir.lib.uwo.ca/wupj/vol2/iss1/13

Chapter 5

1. Merriam Webster's Dictionary

2. psychologytoday.com, Berit Brogard D.M.Sci., Ph.D, Nov 13, 2016, 5 Signs That You're Dealing With a Passive-Aggressive Person,
https://www.psychologytoday.com/us/blog/the-superhuman-mind/201611/5-signs-youre-dealing-passive-aggressive-person

3. psychologytoday.com, Amy Morin, Sep 04, 2015, 9 Things Passive-Aggressive People Do, https://www.psychologytoday.com/us/blog/what-mentally-strong-people-dont-do/201509/9-things-passive-aggressive-people-do

4. See Above #3.

5. CPP Global Human Capital Report, CPP Inc., July 2008, Workplace Conflict, http://img.en25.com/Web/CPP/Conflict_report.pdf

6. High Performance Habits, How Extraordinary People Become That Way, Brendon Burchard, 2017. PP 257-259.

7. http://science.sciencemag.org, Gerardo Ramirez, Sian L. Beilock, 14 JAN 2011 Writing About Testing Worries Boosts Exam Performance in the Classroom, SCIENCE, 14 JAN 2011

: 211-213, http://science.sciencemag.org/content/331/6014/211.
full?sid=0045e680-3e57-43c5-bdfd-d19c563fa6a7

8. Psychiatry Research, Suzanne Jolley, Claire Thompson, James
    Hurley, Evelina Medin, Lucy Butler, Paul Bebbington, Graham
    Dunn, Daniel Freeman, David Fowler, Elizabeth Kuipers,
    Philippa Garety, Jumping to the wrong conclusions? An
    investigation of the mechanisms of reasoning errors in delusions,
    Psychiatry Res. 2014 Oct 30; 219(2): 275–282https://www.
    ncbi.nlm.nih.gov/pmc/articles/PMC4118018/, b.) psychcentral.
    com, Hilary Jacobs Hendel, LCSW, https://psychcentral.com/
    blog/the-benefits-of-not-jumping-to-conclusions/

9. Political Psychology, Volume 39, Issue 1, Nicholas Faulkner,
    02 March 2017, "Put Yourself in Their Shoes": Testing
    Empathy's Ability to Motivate Cosmopolitan Behavior, https://
    onlinelibrary.wiley.com/doi/full/10.1111/pops.12411

10. psychologytoday.com, Hara Estroff Marano, June 9, 2016,The
    Art of the Compliment, https://www.psychologytoday.com/us/
    articles/200403/the-art-the-compliment

Chapter 6

1. a.) Building Effective Relationships in Your Organizations.
       2nd ed, Reina D S, Reina M L. San Francisco, CA: Berrett-
       Koehler; 2006.
    b.) Trust and Betrayal in the Workplace:, Patterson K Grenny
       J McMillan R Switzler
    c.) A Crucial Confrontations: Tools for Resolving Broken
       Promises, Violated Expectations, and Bad Behavior; 2005,
    d.) Overton, A. R., & Lowry, A. C. (2013). Conflict
       Management: Difficult Conversations with Difficult
       People. *Clinics in Colon and Rectal Surgery*, 26(4), 259–264.
       http://doi.org/10.1055/s-0033-1356728, https://www.ncbi.
       nlm.nih.gov/pmc/articles/PMC3835442/

2. The Power of Feedback, John Hattie and Helen Timperley,
    Review of Educational Research March 2007, Vol. 77, No. 1,
    pp. 81–112 DOI: 10.3102/003465430298487

3. foxnews.com, Manuel Alvarez, Outbursts of Explosive Rage: What Causes Them and How Can They Be Prevented?, November 21, 2006, http://www.foxnews.com/story/2006/11/21/outbursts-explosive-rage-what-causes-them-and-how-can-be-prevented.html

4. highconflictinstitute.com, Bill Eddy, LCSW, Esq., 2011, Calming Upset People with EAR https://www.highconflictinstitute.com/free-articles/2018/3/11/calming-upset-people-with-ear

5. A.) www.focusonthefamily.com, Dr. Greg Smalley, Validation is the third step, https://www.focusonthefamily.com/marriage/communication-and-conflict/luve-a-five-step-communication-process-for-conflict-resolution/validation-is-the-third-step-to-conflict-resolution-in-luve,

   B.) MindTools.com, Building Great Work Relationships. https://www.mindtools.com/pages/article/good-relationships.htm

Chapter 7

1. Health.com, Cynthia Saas, MPH, RD, 5 Reasons Most Diets Fail, and How to Succeed, Sept. 30, 2013 https://abcnews.go.com/Health/Wellness/reasons-diets-fail-succeed/story?id=20401440

2. TheDiabetesCouncil.com, Nicole Justus, RN, BSN, 14 Reasons Why Most Diets Fail https://www.thediabetescouncil.com/why-do-most-diets-fail/

3. Inc.com, Ilya Pozin, APR 30, 2016, Here Is Why Confidence Will Always Trump IQ, https://www.inc.com/ilya-pozin/heres-why-confidence-will-always-trump-iq.html, Quoting Tomas Chamorro-Premuzic

4. HBR.org, Thomas Chamorro-Premuzic, May 29, 2013, Can You Really Improve Your Emotional Intelligence? https://hbr.org/2013/05/can-you-really-improve-your-em, 09.25.18

5. JamesClear.com, James Clear, Identity-Based Habits: How to Actually Stick to Your Goals This Year, https://jamesclear.com/identity-based-habits, 8.25.2018

ABOUT THE AUTHOR

Brian Lahoue is a curious lifelong learner with a passion for personal development. His work in both leadership development and entrepreneurship has allowed him the privilege of working with a vast array of individuals from around the globe. Among these are included both young and old, rich and poor, elite and the proletariat, and yet towards all of these with the same goal; to bring out the best within each person, to help each one locate meaning in life, and make the world a better place for all generations.